Eureka

# Eureka

## An Essay on the Material and Spiritual Universe

Edgar Allan Poe

ET REMOTISSIMA PROPE

**100 PAGES**

100 PAGES
Published by Hesperus Press Limited
4 Rickett Street, London SW6 1RU
www.hesperuspress.com

First published as *Eureka, A Prose Poem* by G.P. Putnam, 1848
First published by Hesperus Press Limited, 2002

Foreword © Patrick Moore, 2002

Designed and typeset by Fraser Muggeridge
Printed in the United Arab Emirates by Oriental Press

ISBN: 1-84391-009-8

# CONTENTS

Edgar Allan Poe is remembered as one of the most important literary figures of the early nineteenth century. He had a comparatively short life – he was born in 1809, and died in 1849 – but his contributions were outstanding. It has been said that he more or less created the detective novel; he was a master of the psychological thriller, and also a major poet and author of short stories. In addition he produced perhaps the most influential literary criticism of his time. However, he was not a trained scientist, and this is one reason why *Eureka* is so compelling. Poe was extremely well informed, and he had, of course, a brilliantly imaginative mind.

This 'Essay on the Material and Spiritual Universe' was one of his last works, and it can be dated precisely, because he notes that the ninth asteroid – Flora, one of the small bodies moving round the Sun between the orbits of Mars and Jupiter – was discovered just after the proofs had gone to press. Flora was found in 1848, and Poe died in the following year. Possibly this is Poe's only real contribution to what we now call cosmology; it is not well known, and this new edition is most welcome.

In the introduction, he writes that he will discuss 'the physical, metaphysical and mathematical ... the material and spiritual universe', and add some ideas of his own. The first sections are frankly obscure in places, and Poe may be accused of playing with words, but when he turns to cosmology he introduces concepts which are well ahead of their time. He is not afraid to speculate, or admit his limitations; the mind 'entertains the idea of *limitless*, through the greater difficulty which it finds in entertaining that of *limited*, space'. This is as true today as it was in 1848. To him, the universe is a sphere 'of which the centre is everywhere, the circumference nowhere' – and this, remember, was seventy years before Einstein. He had some idea of an expanding universe: 'absolute unity being taken as a centre ... the universe of stars is the result of radiation from that centre.' Even more significantly, he discusses the force of repulsion. 'The design of the repulsion – the necessity for its existence – I have endeavoured to show, but from all attempt at investigating its nature have religiously abstained.' Einstein introduced his cosmological constant and though he later abandoned it, and described it as the greatest blunder, it is once more under serious consideration. Did Poe anticipate this by a century and a half?

He accepts Sir William Herschel's idea of the shape of the galaxy and speculates about a huge central body: but why 'do we not *see* this vast central sun? At least equal in mass to one hundred million suns such as ours ... it must be non-luminous, as are our planets.' Today we have strong evidence of a supermassive black hole at the galactic centre. Poe could not visualise this, but few astronomers of his time even discussed the concept of a massive central body. He sounds strangely modern too, in discussing clusters of stars: 'The galaxy, let me repeat, is but one of the clusters which I have been describing ... We have no reason to suppose the Milky Way really more extensive than the least of these "nebulae".' Yet fifty years later, the historian Agnes Clerke was still maintaining that the idea of external galaxies was a half-forgotten speculation, and that the Milky Way comprised the entire universe.

Poe's views were not fully confirmed until the work of Edwin Hubble at the Mount Wilson Observatory in 1923. And Poe appreciates that we see the 'clusters' not as they are now, but as they used to be long in the past, because their light has taken 'a vast number of years' to reach us. He introduces what we call Olbers' Paradox – why is it dark at night – and suggests that this may be because the light from very remote objects has not had enough time to reach us. There is a hint of relativity too in his contention that though we regard the galaxy as our own, the same claim may be made for all the other stars in the firmament. We are in no specially privileged position.

In the early nineteenth century the accepted theory of the origin of the Solar system was due to Laplace, and Poe accepts the nebular hypothesis, though he makes some telling modifications of his own. Certainly he was much closer to present-day thinking than Sir James Jeans was in the 1940s, when he championed the idea that the planets were drawn out of the sun by the gravitational action of a passing star. Poe also accepts that there are many stars we cannot see, and that these and other stars may well have planetary systems of the same kind as ours.

In dealing with the spiritual as well as the material aspect, Poe makes another significant point when he seems to go some way toward linking the development of 'vitality' with that of the Earth itself. Admittedly it is rather vague, but it is not impossible that we have here a hint of what is now called the anthropic principle.

All in all, *Eureka* is a fascinating work. It throws new light on Poe himself; had he lived longer, or had he not been so preoccupied with purely literary work, he might have made very valuable contributions to the understanding of the universe. Read this 'essay' carefully; there is much more to it than meets the eye.

*– Sir Patrick Moore, 2002*

# Eureka

*With very profound respect this work is dedicated
to Alexander von Humboldt*

To the few who love me and whom I love, to those who feel rather than think, to the dreamers and those who put their faith in dreams as in the only realities, I offer this book of truths, not in its character of truth-teller, but for the beauty that abounds in its truth, constituting it true. To these I present the composition as an art product alone – let us say as a romance – or, if I be not urging too lofty a claim, as a poem.

What I here propound is true, therefore it cannot die; or if by any means it be now trodden down so that it die, it will 'rise again to the life everlasting'.

Nevertheless, it is as a poem only that I wish this work to be judged after I am dead.

*– Edgar Allan Poe*

It is with humility really unassumed, it is with a sentiment even of awe, that I pen the opening sentence of this work: for of all conceivable subjects, I approach the reader with the most solemn, the most comprehensive, the most difficult, the most august.

What terms shall I find sufficiently simple in their sublimity, sufficiently sublime in their simplicity, for the mere enunciation of my theme?

I design to speak of the physical, metaphysical and mathematical – of the material and spiritual universe; of its essence, its origin, its creation, its present condition, and its destiny. I shall be so rash, moreover, as to challenge the conclusions, and thus, in effect, to question the sagacity of many of the greatest and most justly reverenced of men.

In the beginning, let me as distinctly as possible announce, not the theorem which I hope to demonstrate – for, whatever the mathematicians may assert, there is, in this world at least, no such thing as demonstration – but the ruling idea which, throughout this volume, I shall be continually endeavouring to suggest.

My general proposition, then, is this: in the original unity of the first thing lies the secondary cause of all things, with the germ of their inevitable annihilation.

In illustration of this idea, I propose to take such a survey of the universe that the mind may be able really to receive and to perceive an individual impression.

He who from the top of Etna casts his eyes leisurely around is affected chiefly by the extent and diversity of the scene. Only by a rapid whirling on his heel could he hope to comprehend the panorama in the sublimity of its oneness. But as, on the summit of Etna, no man has thought of whirling on his heel, so no man has ever taken into his brain the full uniqueness of the prospect; and so, again, whatever considerations lie involved in this uniqueness, have as yet no practical existence for mankind.

I do not know a treatise in which a survey of the universe – using the word in its most comprehensive and only legitimate acceptation – is taken at all, and it may be as well here to mention that by the term 'universe', wherever employed without

5

qualification in this essay, I mean, in most cases, to designate the utmost conceivable expanse of space, with all things, spiritual and material, that can be imagined to exist within the compass of that expanse. In speaking of what is ordinarily implied by the expression 'universe', I shall take a phrase of limitation: 'the universe of stars'. Why this distinction is considered necessary will be seen in the sequel.

But even of treatises on the really limited, although always assumed as the unlimited, universe of stars, I know none in which a survey, even of this limited universe, is so taken as to warrant deductions from its individuality. The nearest approach to such a work is made in the *Cosmos* of Alexander von Humboldt. He presents the subject, however, not in its individuality but in its generality. His theme, in its last result, is the law of *each* portion of the merely physical universe, as this law is related to the laws of *every other* portion of this merely physical universe. His design is simply synoeretical. In a word, he discusses the universality of material relation, and discloses to the eye of philosophy whatever inferences have hitherto lain hidden behind this universality. But however admirable be the succinctness with which he has treated each particular point of his topic, the mere multiplicity of these points occasions, necessarily, an amount of detail, and thus an involution of idea, which preclude all individuality of impression.

It seems to me that, in aiming at this latter effect, and, through it, at the consequences – the conclusions, the suggestions, the speculations, or, if nothing better offer itself, the mere guesses – which may result from it, we require something like a mental gyration on the heel. We need so rapid a revolution of all things about the central point of sight that, while the minutiae vanish altogether, even the more conspicuous objects become blended into one. Among the vanishing minutiae, in a survey of this kind, would be all exclusively terrestrial matters. The Earth would be considered in its planetary relations alone. A man, in this view, becomes mankind; mankind a member of the cosmic family of intelligences.

And now, before proceeding to our subject proper, let me beg the reader's attention to an extract or two from a somewhat remarkable letter, which appears to have been found corked in a bottle and floating on the *Mare Tenebrarum* – an ocean well described by the Nubian geographer, Ptolemy Hephestion, but little frequented in modern days unless by the transcendentalists and some other divers for crotchets. The date of this letter, I confess, surprises me even more particularly than its contents, for it seems to have been written in the year two thousand eight hundred and forty eight. As for the passages I am about to transcribe, they, I fancy, will speak for themselves.

*'Do you know, my dear friend,'* says the writer, addressing, no doubt, a contemporary, *'Do you know that it is scarcely more than eight or nine hundred years ago since the metaphysicians first consented to relieve the people of the singular fancy that there exist but two practicable roads to Truth? Believe it if you can! It appears, however, that long, long ago, in the night of time, there lived a Turkish philosopher called Aries and surnamed Tottle.'* [Here, possibly, the letter-writer means Aristotle; the best names are wretchedly corrupted in two or three thousand years.] *'The fame of this great man depended mainly upon his demonstration that sneezing is a natural provision, by means of which over-profound thinkers are enabled to expel superfluous ideas through the nose; but he obtained a scarcely less valuable celebrity as the founder, or at all events as the principal propagator, of what was termed the deductive or a-priori philosophy. He started with what he maintained to be axioms, or self-evident truths, and the now well-understood fact that no truths are self-evident really does not make in the slightest degree against his speculations. It was sufficient for his purpose that the truths in question were evident at all. From axioms he proceeded, logically, to results. His most illustrious disciples were one Tuclid, a geometrician* [meaning Euclid], *and one Kant, a Dutchman, the originator of that species of Transcendentalism which, with the change merely of a C for a K, now bears his peculiar name.*

*'Well, Aries Tottle flourished supreme, until the advent of one*

Hog, surnamed "the Ettrick shepherd", who preached an entirely different system, which he called the a posteriori or inductive. His plan referred altogether to sensation. He proceeded by observing, analysing, and classifying facts – instantiae Naturae as they were somewhat affectedly called – and arranging them into general laws. In a word, while the mode of Aries rested on noumena, that of Hog depended on phenomena, and so great was the admiration excited by this latter system that, at its first introduction, Aries fell into general disrepute. Finally, however, he recovered ground, and was permitted to divide the empire of philosophy with his more modern rival; the savants contenting themselves with proscribing all other competitors, past, present, and to come, putting an end to all controversy on the topic by the promulgation of a Median law, to the effect that the Aristotelian and Baconian roads are, and of right ought to be, the sole possible avenues to knowledge. "Baconian", you must know, my dear friend,' adds the letter-writer at this point, 'was an adjective invented as equivalent to Hogian, and at the same time more dignified and euphonious.

'Now I do assure you most positively,' proceeds the epistle, 'that I represent these matters fairly. And you can easily understand how restrictions so absurd on their very face must have operated, in those days, to retard the progress of true science, which makes its most important advances, as all history will show, by seemingly intuitive leaps. These ancient ideas confined investigation to crawling, and I need not suggest to you that crawling, among varieties of locomotion, is a very capital thing of its kind. But because the snail is sure of foot, for this reason must we clip the wings of the eagles? For many centuries so great was the infatuation, about Hog especially, that a virtual stop was put to all thinking, properly so called. No man dared utter a truth for which he felt himself indebted to his soul alone. It mattered not whether the truth was even demonstrably such, for the dogmatising philosophers of that epoch regarded only the road by which it professed to have been attained. The end, with them, was a point of no moment whatever: "The means!" they vociferated, "let us look at the means!" And if, on scrutiny of the means, it was found to *come neither under the category Hog, nor under the category Aries (which means ram), why then the savants went no further. Calling the thinker a fool and branding him a "theorist", they would never, thereafter, have anything to do either with him or with his truths.*

*'Now, my dear friend,'* continues the letter-writer, *'it cannot be maintained that, by the crawling system exclusively adopted, men would arrive at the maximum amount of truth, even in any long series of ages, for the repression of imagination was an evil not to be counterbalanced even by absolute certainty in the snail processes. But their certainty was very far from absolute. The error of our progenitors was quite analogous with that of the wiseacre who fancies he must necessarily see an object the more distinctly, the more closely he holds it to his eyes. They blinded themselves, too, with the impalpable, titillating Scotch snuff of detail. And thus the boasted facts of the Hogites were by no means always facts – a point of little importance but for the assumption that they always* were. *The vital taint, however, in Baconianism – its most lamentable fount of error – lay in its tendency to throw power and consideration into the hands of merely perceptive men, of those inter-Tritonic minnows, the microscopic savants, the diggers and peddlers of minute facts, for the most part in physical science, facts all of which they retailed at the same price upon the highway, their value depending, it was supposed, simply upon the fact of their fact, without reference to their applicability or inapplicability in the development of those ultimate and only legitimate facts, called Law.*

*'Than the persons,'* the letter goes on to say, *'than the persons thus suddenly elevated by the Hogian philosophy into a station for which they were unfitted, thus transferred from the sculleries into the parlours of science, from its pantries into its pulpits; than these individuals, a more intolerant, a more intolerable set of bigots and tyrants never existed on the face of the Earth. Their creed, their text, and their sermon were alike – the one word 'fact'. But, for the most part, even of this one word they knew not even the meaning. On those who ventured to disturb their facts with the view of*

putting them in order and to use, the disciples of Hog had no mercy whatever. All attempts at generalisation were met at once by the words, 'theoretical', 'theory', 'theorist'; all thought, to be brief, was very properly resented as a personal affront to themselves. Cultivating the natural sciences to the exclusion of metaphysics, the mathematics, and logic, many of these Bacon-engendered philosophers – one-ideaed, one-sided, and lame of a leg – were more wretchedly helpless, more miserably ignorant, in view of all the comprehensible objects of knowledge, than the veriest unlettered hind who proves that he knows something at least in admitting that he knows absolutely nothing.

'Nor had our forefathers any better right to talk about certainty when pursuing, in blind confidence, the a-priori path of axioms, or of the Ram. At innumerable points this path was scarcely as straight as a ram's horn. The simple truth is that the Aristotelians erected their castles upon a basis far less reliable than air, for no such things as axioms ever existed or can possibly exist at all. This they must have been very blind indeed not to see, or at least to suspect, for, even in their own day, many of their long-admitted 'axioms' had been abandoned: "ex nihilo nihil fit", for example, and a "thing cannot act where it is not", and "there cannot be antipodes", and "darkness cannot proceed from light". These and numerous similar propositions formerly accepted, without hesitation, as axioms, or undeniable truths, were, even at the period of which I speak, seen to be altogether untenable. How absurd in these people, then, to persist in relying upon a basis as immutable, whose mutability had become so repeatedly manifest!

'But, even through evidence afforded by themselves against themselves, it is easy to convict these a-priori reasoners of the grossest unreason; it is easy to show the futility, the impalpability, of their axioms in general. I have now lying before me,' it will be observed that we still proceed with the letter, 'I have now lying before me a book printed about a thousand years ago. Pundit assures me that it is decidedly the cleverest ancient work on its topic, which is "Logic". The author, who was much esteemed in his day, was one Miller, or Mill, and we find it recorded of him, as a point of some importance, that he rode a mill-horse whom he called Jeremy Bentham. But let us glance at the volume itself.

'Ah! "Ability or inability to conceive," says Mr Mill, very properly, "is in no case to be received as a criterion of axiomatic truth." Now, that this is a palpable truism no one in his senses will deny. Not to admit the proposition is to insinuate a charge of variability in truth itself, whose very title is a synonym of the steadfast. If ability to conceive be taken as a criterion of truth, then a truth to David Hume would very seldom be a truth to Joe, and ninety-nine hundredths of what is undeniable in Heaven would be demonstrable falsity upon Earth. The proposition of Mr Mill, then, is sustained. I will not grant it to be an axiom, and this merely because I am showing that no axioms exist. But, with a distinction which could not have been cavilled at even by Mr Mill himself, I am ready to grant that if an axiom there be, then the proposition of which we speak has the fullest right to be considered an axiom – that no more absolute axiom is. And, consequently, that any subsequent proposition which shall conflict with this one primarily advanced must be either a falsity in itself – that is to say, no axiom – or, if admitted axiomatic, must at once neutralise both itself and its predecessor.

'And now, by the logic of their own propounder, let us proceed to test any one of the axioms propounded. Let us give Mr Mill the fairest of play. We will bring the point to no ordinary issue. We will select for investigation no commonplace axiom – no axiom of what, not the less preposterously because only impliedly, he terms his secondary class – as if a positive truth by definition could be either more or less positively a truth. We will select, I say, no axiom of an unquestionability so questionable as is to be found in Euclid. We will not talk, for example, about such propositions as that two straight lines cannot enclose a space, or that the whole is greater than any one of its parts. We will afford the logician every advantage. We will come at once to a proposition which he regards as the acme of the unquestionable, as the quintessence of axiomatic undeniability. Here it is: "Contradictions cannot both be true, that is, cannot coexist in nature."

'Here Mr Mill means, for instance, and I give the most forcible instance conceivable, that a tree must be either a tree or not a tree – that it cannot be at the same time a tree and not a tree. All which is quite reasonable of itself, and will answer remarkably well as an axiom, until we bring it into collation with an axiom insisted upon a few pages before; in other words – words which I have previously employed – until we test it by the logic of its own propounder. "A tree," Mr Mill asserts, "must be either a tree or not a tree." Very well. And now let me ask him, why? To this little query there is but one response. I defy any man living to invent a second. The sole answer is this: "Because we find it impossible to conceive that a tree can be anything else than a tree or not a tree."

'This, I repeat, is Mr Mill's sole answer. He will not pretend to suggest another, and yet, by his own showing, his answer is clearly no answer at all, for has he not already required us to admit, as an axiom, that ability or inability to conceive is in no case to be taken as a criterion of axiomatic truth? Thus all, absolutely all, his argumentation is at sea without a rudder. Let it not be urged that an exception from the general rule is to be made in cases where the "impossibility to conceive" is so peculiarly great as when we are called upon to conceive a tree both a tree and not a tree. Let no attempt, I say, be made at urging this 'sotticism', for, in the first place, there are no degrees of 'impossibility', and thus no one impossible conception can be more peculiarly impossible than another impossible conception; in the second place, Mr Mill himself, no doubt after thorough deliberation, has most distinctly and most rationally excluded all opportunity for exception by the emphasis of his proposition, that, in no case, is ability or inability to conceive to be taken as a criterion of axiomatic truth; in the third place, even were exceptions admissible at all, it remains to be shown how any exception is admissible here. That a tree can be both a tree and not a tree is an idea which the angels, or the devils, may entertain, and which no doubt many an earthly Bedlamite, or transcendentalist, does.

'Now I do not quarrel with these ancients,' continues the letter-writer, 'so much on account of the transparent frivolity of their logic – which, to be plain, was baseless, worthless, and fantastic altogether – as on account of their pompous and infatuate proscription of all other roads to Truth than the two narrow and crooked paths, the one of creeping and the other of crawling, to which, in their ignorant perversity, they have dared to confine the soul – the soul which loves nothing so well as to soar in those regions of illimitable intuition which are utterly incognisant of "path".

'By the by, my dear friend, is it not an evidence of the mental slavery entailed upon those bigoted people by their Hogs and Rams, that, in spite of the eternal prating of their savants about roads to Truth, none of them fell, even by accident, into what we now so distinctly perceive to be the broadest, the straightest, and most available of all mere roads – the great thoroughfare, the majestic highway of the consistent? Is it not wonderful that they should have failed to deduce from the works of God the vitally momentous consideration that a perfect consistency can be nothing but an absolute truth? How plain, how rapid our progress since the late announcement of this proposition! By its means, investigation has been taken out of the hands of the ground moles, and given as a duty, rather than as a task, to the true, to the only true thinkers, to the generally educated men of ardent imagination. These latter – our Keplers, our Laplaces – "speculate", "theorise"; these are the terms. Can you not fancy the shout of scorn with which they would be received by our progenitors were it possible for them to be looking over my shoulders as I write? The Keplers, I repeat, speculate, theorise, and their theories are merely corrected – reduced – sifted – cleared, little by little, of their chaff of inconsistency, until at length there stands apparent an unencumbered consistency, a consistency which the most stolid admit, because it is a consistency, to be an absolute and unquestionable truth.

'I have often thought, my friend, that it must have puzzled these dogmaticians of a thousand years ago to determine, even, by which of their two boasted roads it is that the cryptographist attains the solution of the more complicated ciphers. Or by which of them Champollion guided mankind to those important and *innumerable truths which, for so many centuries, have lain entombed amid the phonetic hieroglyphics of Egypt. In special, would it not have given these bigots some trouble to determine by which of their two roads was reached the most momentous and sublime of all their truths – the truth, the fact, of gravitation? Newton deduced it from the laws of Kepler. Kepler admitted that these laws he* guessed *– these laws whose investigation disclosed to the greatest of British astronomers that principle, the basis of all (existing) physical principles, in going behind which we enter at once the nebulous kingdom of metaphysics. Yes! These vital laws Kepler* guessed, *that it is to say, he* imagined *them. Had he been asked to point out either the deductive or inductive route by which he attained them, his reply might have been, "I know nothing about routes, but I do know the machinery of the universe. Here it is. I grasped it with my soul, I reached it through mere dint of intuition." Alas, poor ignorant old man! Could not any metaphysician have told him that what he called "intuition" was but the conviction resulting from deductions or inductions, of which the processes were so shadowy as to have escaped his consciousness, eluded his reason, or bidden defiance to his capacity of expression? How great a pity it is that some "moral philosopher" had not enlightened him about all this! How it would have comforted him on his deathbed to know that, instead of having gone intuitively and thus unbecomingly, he had, in fact, proceeded decorously and legitimately – that is to say, Hogishly, or at least Ramishly – into the vast halls where lay gleaming, untended, and hitherto untouched by mortal hand, unseen by mortal eye, the imperishable and priceless secrets of the universe!*

'*Yes, Kepler was essentially a theorist. But this title, now of so much sanctity, was, in those ancient days, a designation of supreme contempt. It is only now that men begin to appreciate that divine old man, to sympathise with the prophetical and poetical rhapsody of his ever-memorable words. For my part,*' continues the unknown correspondent, '*I glow with a sacred fire when I even think of them, and feel that I shall never grow weary of their repetition. In concluding this letter, let me have the real pleasure of transcribing them once again:* "I care not whether my work be read now or by posterity. I can afford to wait a century for readers when God himself has waited six thousand years for an observer. I triumph. I have stolen the golden secret of the Egyptians. I will indulge my sacred fury." '

Here end my quotations from this very unaccountable if not impertinent epistle, and perhaps it would be folly to comment, in any respect, upon the chimerical, not to say revolutionary, fancies of the writer – whoever he is – fancies so radically at war with the well-considered and well-settled opinions of this age. Let us proceed, then, to our legitimate thesis, the universe.

This thesis admits a choice between two modes of discussion: we may ascend or descend. Beginning at our own point of view, at the Earth on which we stand, we may pass to the other planets of our system, thence to the Sun, thence to our system considered collectively, and thence, through other systems, indefinitely outwards. Or, commencing on high at some point as definite as we can make or conceive it, we may come down to the habitation of man. Usually, that is to say, in ordinary essays on astronomy, the first of these two modes is, with certain reservations, adopted. This for the obvious reason that astronomical facts, merely, and principles, being the object, that object is best fulfilled in stepping from the known because proximate, gradually onward to the point where all certitude becomes lost in the remote. For my present purpose, however, that of enabling the mind to take in, as if from afar and at one glance, a distant conception of the individual universe, it is clear that a descent to small from great – to the outskirts from the centre (if we could establish a centre) – to the end from the beginning (if we could fancy a beginning) – would be the preferable course, but for the difficulty, if not impossibility, of presenting in this course to the unastronomical a picture at all comprehensible in regard to such considerations as are involved in quantity, that is to say, in number, magnitude, and distance.

Now, distinctness, intelligibility, at all points is a primary feature in my general design. On important topics it is better to be a good deal prolix than even a very little obscure. But abstruseness is a quality appertaining to no subject in itself. All are alike, in facility of comprehension, to him who approaches them by properly graduated steps. It is merely because a stepping-stone, here and there, is heedlessly left unsupplied in our road to the differential calculus, that this latter is not altogether as simple a thing as a sonnet by Mr Solomon Seesaw.

By way of admitting, then, no chance for misapprehension, I think it advisable to proceed as if even the more obvious facts of astronomy were unknown to the reader. In combining the two modes of discussion to which I have referred, I propose to avail myself of the advantages peculiar to each, and very specially of the iteration in detail which will be unavoidable as a consequence of the plan. Commencing with a descent, I shall reserve for the return upwards those indispensable considerations of quantity to which allusion has already been made.

Let us begin, then, at once, with that merest of words: 'infinity'. This, like 'God', 'spirit', and some other expressions of which the equivalents exist in all languages, is by no means the expression of an idea, but of an effort at one. It stands for the possible attempt at an impossible conception. Man needed a term by which to point out the direction of this effort – the cloud behind which lay, forever invisible, the object of this attempt. A word, in fine, was demanded, by means of which one human being might put himself in relation at once with another human being and with a certain tendency of the human intellect. Out of this demand arose the word 'infinity', which is thus the representative but of the thought of a thought.

As regards *that* infinity now considered – the infinity of space – we often hear it said that 'its idea is admitted by the mind, is acquiesced in, is entertained, on account of the greater difficulty which attends the conception of a limit'. But this is merely one of those phrases by which even profound thinkers, time out of mind, have occasionally taken pleasure in deceiving themselves. The quibble lies concealed in the word 'difficulty'. 'The mind,' we are told, 'entertains the idea of *limitless*, through the greater

difficulty which it finds in entertaining that of *limited*, space.'
Now, were the proposition but fairly put, its absurdity would
become transparent at once. Clearly, there is no mere difficulty in
the case. The assertion intended, if presented according to its
intention, and without sophistry, would run thus: 'The mind
admits the idea of limitless, through the greater *impossibility* of
entertaining that of limited, space.'

It must be immediately seen that this is not a question of
two statements between whose respective credibilities, or of
two arguments between whose respective validities, the reason is
called upon to decide; it is a matter of two conceptions, directly
conflicting, and each avowedly impossible, one of which the
intellect is supposed to be capable of entertaining, on account of
the greater impossibility of entertaining the other. The choice is
not made between two difficulties; it is merely *fancied* to be made
between two impossibilities. Now of the former there are degrees,
but of the latter none, just as our impertinent letter-writer has
already suggested. A task may be more or less difficult, but it is
either possible or not possible – there are no gradations. It might
be more *difficult* to overthrow the Andes than an anthill, but it
can be no more *impossible* to annihilate the matter of the one than
the matter of the other. A man may jump ten feet with less
*difficulty* than he can jump twenty, but the *impossibility* of his
leaping to the moon is not a whit less than that of his leaping to
the dog-star.

Since all this is undeniable, since the choice of the mind is to
be made between impossibilities of conception, since one
impossibility cannot be greater than another, and since, thus, one
cannot be preferred to another, the philosophers who not only
maintain, on the grounds mentioned, man's *idea* of infinity but,
on account of such supposititious idea, *infinity itself*, are plainly
engaged in demonstrating one impossible thing to be possible by
showing how it is that some one other thing is impossible too.
This, it will be said, is nonsense, and perhaps it is. Indeed I think
it very capital nonsense, but forego all claim to it as nonsense of
mine.

The readiest mode, however, of displaying the fallacy of the philosophical argument on this question is by simply adverting to a fact respecting it which has been hitherto quite overlooked – the fact that the argument alluded to both proves and disproves its own proposition. 'The mind is impelled,' say the theologians and others, 'to admit a first cause, by the superior difficulty it experiences in conceiving cause beyond cause without end.' The quibble, as before, lies in the word 'difficulty', but here, what is it employed to sustain? A first cause. And what is a first cause? An ultimate termination of causes. And what is an ultimate termination of causes? Finity – the finite. Thus the one quibble, in two processes, by God knows how many philosophers, is made to support now finity and now infinity; could it not be brought to support something besides? As for the quibbles, they, at least, are insupportable. But, to dismiss them: what they prove in the one case is the identical nothing which they demonstrate in the other.

Of course, no one will suppose that I here contend for the absolute impossibility of that which we attempt to convey in the word 'infinity'. My purpose is but to show the folly of endeavouring to prove infinity itself, or even our conception of it, by any such blundering ratiocination as that which is ordinarily employed.

Nevertheless, as an individual, I may be permitted to say that I cannot conceive infinity, and am convinced that no human being can. A mind not thoroughly self-conscious, not accustomed to the introspective analysis of its own operations, will, it is true, often deceive itself by supposing that it *has* entertained the conception of which we speak. In the effort to entertain it, we proceed step beyond step, we fancy point still beyond point, and so long as we continue the effort, it may be said, in fact, that we are tending to the formation of the idea designed, while the strength of the impression that we actually form or have formed it, is in the ratio of the period during which we keep up the mental endeavour. But it is in the act of discontinuing the endeavour, of fulfilling (as we think) the idea, of putting the finishing stroke (as we suppose) to the conception, that we overthrow at once the whole fabric of our fancy by resting upon some one ultimate, and therefore definite, point. This fact, however, we fail to perceive on account of the absolute coincidence, in time, between the settling down upon the ultimate point and the act of cessation in thinking. In attempting, on the other hand, to frame the idea of a limited space, we merely converse the processes which involve the impossibility.

We believe in a God. We may or may not believe in finite or in infinite space, but our belief, in such cases, is more properly designated as faith, and is a matter quite distinct from that belief proper – from that intellectual belief – which presupposes the mental conception.

The fact is that upon the enunciation of any one of that class of terms to which 'infinity' belongs – the class representing thoughts of thought – he who has a right to say that he thinks at all, feels himself called upon not to entertain a conception but simply to direct his mental vision toward some given point in the intellectual firmament, where lies a nebula never to be resolved. To solve it, indeed, he makes no effort, for with a rapid instinct he comprehends not only the impossibility but, as regards all human purposes, the inessentiality of its solution. He perceives that the deity has not designed it to be solved. He sees, at once, that it lies out of the brain of man, and even *how*, if not exactly *why*, it lies out of it. There are people, I am aware, who, busying themselves in attempts at the unattainable, acquire very easily, by dint of the jargon they emit, among those thinkers-that-they-think with whom darkness and depth are synonymous, a kind of cuttlefish reputation for profundity. But the finest quality of thought is its self-cognisance, and, with some little equivocation, it may be said that no fog of the mind can well be greater than that which, extending to the very boundaries of the mental domain, shuts out even these boundaries themselves from comprehension.

It will now be understood that in using the phrase, 'infinity of space', I make no call upon the reader to entertain the impossible conception of an absolute infinity. I refer simply to the 'utmost conceivable expanse' of space – a shadowy and fluctuating domain, now shrinking, now swelling, with the vacillating energies of the imagination.

Hitherto, the universe of stars has always been considered as coincident with the universe proper, as I have defined it in the commencement of this discourse. It has been always either directly or indirectly assumed, at least since the dawn of intelligible astronomy, that were it possible for us to attain any given point in space we should still find, on all sides of us, an interminable succession of stars. This was the untenable idea of Pascal when making perhaps the most successful attempt ever made, at periphrasing the conception for which we struggle in the word 'universe'. 'It is a sphere,' he says, 'of which the centre is everywhere, the circumference nowhere.' But although this intended definition is, in fact, no definition of the universe of stars, we may accept it, with some mental reservation, as a definition (rigorous enough for all practical purposes) of the universe proper – that is to say, of the universe of space. This latter, then, let us regard as 'a sphere of which the centre is everywhere, the circumference nowhere'. In fact, while we find it impossible to fancy an end to space, we have no difficulty in picturing to ourselves any one of an infinity of beginnings.

As our starting-point, then, let us adopt the Godhead. Of this Godhead, in itself, he alone is not imbecile, he alone is not impious who propounds – nothing. '*Nous ne connaissons rien,*' says the Baron de Bielfeld. '*Nous ne connaissons rien de la nature ou de l'essence de Dieu: pour savoir ce qu'il est, il faut être Dieu même.*' 'We know absolutely nothing of the nature or essence of God: in order to comprehend what He is, we should have to be God ourselves.'

'*We should have to be God ourselves!*' With a phrase so startling as this yet ringing in my ears, I nevertheless venture to demand if this our present ignorance of the deity is an ignorance to which the soul is everlastingly condemned.

By Him, however – now, at least, the incomprehensible – by Him, assuming Him as spirit, that is to say, as not matter, a distinction which, for all intelligible purposes, will stand well

20

instead of a definition – by Him, then, existing as spirit, let us content ourselves with supposing to have been created, or made out of nothing, by dint of His volition, at some point of space which we will take as a centre, at some period into which we do not pretend to enquire, but at all events immensely remote – by Him, then again, let us suppose to have been created – *what*? This is a vitally momentous epoch in our considerations. *What* is it that we are justified, that alone we are justified, in supposing to have been primarily created?

We have attained a point where only intuition can aid us. But now let me recur to the idea which I have already suggested as that alone which we can properly entertain of intuition. It is but the conviction arising from those inductions or deductions of which the processes are so shadowy as to escape our consciousness, elude our reason, or defy our capacity of expression. With this understanding, I now assert that an intuition altogether irresistible, although inexpressible, forces me to the conclusion that what God originally created – that that matter which, by dint of His volition, He first made from His spirit, or from nihility, could have been nothing but matter in its utmost conceivable state of – what? – of simplicity.

This will be found the sole absolute assumption of my discourse. I use the word 'assumption' in its ordinary sense, yet I maintain that even this my primary proposition is very far indeed from being really a mere assumption. Nothing was ever more certainly – no human conclusion was ever, in fact, more regularly – more rigorously deduced. But, alas! The processes lie out of the human analysis – at all events are beyond the utterance of the human tongue. If, however, in the course of this essay I succeed in showing that out of matter in its extreme of simplicity all things *might* have been, we reach directly the inference that they *were*, thus constructed, through the impossibility of attributing supererogation to omnipotence.

Let us now endeavour to conceive what matter must be, when, or if, in its absolute extreme of simplicity. Here the reason flies at once to imparticularity – to a particle – to *one* particle – a particle of *one* kind – of *one* character – of *one* nature – of *one* size – of *one* form – a particle, therefore, 'without form and void' – a particle positively a particle at all points – a particle absolutely unique, individual, undivided, and not indivisible only because He who created it by dint of His will can by an infinitely less energetic exercise of the same will, as a matter of course, divide it.

Oneness, then, is all that I predicate of the originally created matter; but I propose to show that this oneness is a principle abundantly sufficient to account for the constitution, the existing phenomena, and the plainly inevitable annihilation, of at least the material universe.

The willing into being the primordial particle has completed the act, or more properly the conception, of creation. We now proceed to the ultimate purpose for which we are to suppose the particle created – that is to say, the ultimate purpose so far as our considerations yet enable us to see it – the constitution of the universe from it, the particle.

This constitution has been effected by forcing the originally and therefore normally one into the abnormal condition of many. An action of this character implies reaction. A diffusion from unity, under the conditions, involves a tendency to return into unity – a tendency ineradicable until satisfied. But on these points I will speak more fully hereafter.

The assumption of absolute unity in the primordial particle includes that of infinite divisibility.[1] Let us conceive the particle, then, to be only not totally exhausted by diffusion into space. From the one particle, as a centre, let us suppose to be radiated spherically, in all directions, to immeasurable but still definite distances in the previously vacant space, a certain inexpressibly great yet limited number of unimaginably yet not infinitely minute atoms.

Now, of these atoms, thus diffused, or upon diffusion, what conditions are we permitted, not to assume, but to infer, from consideration as well of their source as of the character of the design apparent in their diffusion? Unity being their source, and difference from unity the character of the design manifested in their diffusion, we are warranted in supposing this character to be at least generally preserved throughout the design, and to form a portion of the design itself; that is to say, we shall be warranted in conceiving continual differences at all points from the uniquity and simplicity of the origin. But, for these reasons, shall we be justified in imagining the atoms heterogeneous, dissimilar, unequal, and inequidistant? More explicitly, are we to consider no two atoms as, at their diffusion, of the same nature or of the same form or of the same size? And, after fulfilment of their diffusion into space, is absolute inequidistance, each from each, to be understood of all of them? In such arrangement, under such conditions, we most easily and immediately comprehend the subsequent most feasible carrying out to completion of any such design as that which I have suggested – the design of variety out of unity – diversity out of sameness – heterogeneity out of homogeneity – complexity out of simplicity – in a word, the utmost possible multiplicity of relation out of the emphatically irrelative one. Undoubtedly, therefore, we *should* be warranted in assuming all that has been mentioned but for the reflection, first, that supererogation is not presumable of any divine act; and, secondly, that the object supposed in view appears as feasible when some of the conditions in question are dispensed with in the beginning, as when all are understood immediately to exist. I mean to say that some are involved in the rest, or so instantaneous a consequence of them as to make the distinction inappreciable. Difference of size, for example, will at once be brought about through the tendency of one atom to a second, in preference to a third, on account of particular inequidistance, which is to be comprehended as particular inequidistances between centres of quantity, in neighbouring atoms of different form – a matter not at all interfering with the generally equable distribution of the atoms. Difference of kind, too, is easily conceived to be merely a result of differences in size and form, taken more or less conjointly. In fact, since the unity of the particle proper implies absolute homogeneity, we cannot imagine the atoms, at their diffusion, differing in kind without imagining, at the same time, a special exercise of the divine will at the emission of each atom, for the purpose of effecting in each a change of its essential nature. And so fantastic an idea is the less to be indulged as the object proposed is seen to be thoroughly attainable without such minute and elaborate interposition. We perceive, therefore, upon the whole, that it would be supererogatory, and consequently unphilosophical, to predicate of the atoms, in view of their purposes, anything more than difference of form at their dispersion, with particular inequidistance after it – all other differences arising at once out of these, in the very first processes of mass-constitution. We thus establish the universe on a purely geometrical basis. Of course, it is by no means necessary to assume absolute difference, even of form, among all the atoms radiated, any more than absolute particular inequidistance of each from each. We are required to conceive merely that no neighbouring atoms are of similar form – no atoms which can ever approximate, until their inevitable reunion at the end.

Although the immediate and perpetual tendency of the disunited atoms to return into their normal unity is implied, as I have said, in their abnormal diffusion, still it is clear that this tendency will be without consequence – a tendency and no more – until the diffusive energy, in ceasing to be exerted, shall leave it, the tendency, free to seek its satisfaction. The divine act, however, being considered as determinate, and discontinued on fulfilment of the diffusion, we understand, at once, a reaction – in other words, a *satisfiable* tendency of the disunited atoms to return into one.

But the diffusive energy being withdrawn, and the reaction having commenced in furtherance of the ultimate design – that of the utmost possible relation – this design is now in danger of being frustrated, in detail, by reason of that very tendency to return which is to effect its accomplishment in general. Multiplicity is the object; but there is nothing to prevent proximate atoms from lapsing at once, through the now satisfiable tendency, *before* the fulfilment of any ends proposed in multiplicity, into absolute oneness among themselves. There is nothing to impede the aggregation of various unique masses, at various points of space – in other words, nothing to interfere with the accumulation of various masses, each absolutely one.

For the effectual completion of the general design, we thus see the necessity for a repulsion of limited capacity – a separate something which, on withdrawal of the diffusive volition, shall at the same time allow the approach and forbid the junction of the atoms, suffering them infinitely to approximate, while denying them positive contact. In a word, having the power, up to a certain epoch, of preventing their coalition, but no ability to interfere with their coalescence in any respect or degree. The repulsion, already considered as so peculiarly limited in other regards, must be understood, let me repeat, as having power to prevent absolute coalition, only up to a certain epoch. Unless we are to conceive that the appetite for unity among the atoms is doomed to be satisfied *never*; unless we are to conceive that what had a beginning is to have no end – a conception which cannot really be entertained, however much we may talk or dream of entertaining it – we are forced to conclude that the repulsive influence imagined will, finally, under pressure of the uni-tendency collectively applied, but never and in no degree until, on fulfilment of the divine purposes, such collective application shall be naturally made, yield to a force which, at that ultimate epoch, shall be the superior force precisely to the extent required, and thus permit the universal subsidence into the inevitable, because original and therefore normal, one. The conditions here to be reconciled are difficult indeed; we cannot even comprehend the possibility of their conciliation. Nevertheless, the apparent impossibility is brilliantly suggestive.

That the repulsive something actually exists, we see. Man neither employs, nor knows, a force sufficient to bring two atoms into contact. This is but the well-established proposition of the impenetrability of matter. All experiment proves, all philosophy admits it. The design of the repulsion – the necessity for its existence – I have endeavoured to show, but from all attempt at investigating its nature have religiously abstained; this on account of an intuitive conviction that the principle at issue is strictly spiritual – lies in a recess impervious to our present understanding; lies involved in a consideration of what now, in our human state, is *not* to be considered – in a consideration of spirit in itself. I feel, in a word, that here the God has interposed, and here only, because here and here only the knot demanded the interposition of the God.

In fact, while the tendency of the diffused atoms to return into unity will be recognised, at once, as the principle of the Newtonian gravity, what I have spoken of as a repulsive influence prescribing limits to the (immediate) satisfaction of the tendency will be understood as that which we have been in the practice of designating now as heat, now as magnetism, now as electricity, displaying our ignorance of its awful character in the vacillation of the phraseology with which we endeavour to circumscribe it.

Calling it, merely for the moment, electricity, we know that all experimental analysis of electricity has given, as an ultimate result, the principle, or seeming principle, heterogeneity. Only where things differ is electricity apparent; and it is presumable that they never differ where it is not developed at least, if not apparent. Now, this result is in the fullest keeping with that which I have reached unempirically. The design of the repulsive influence I have suggested to be that of preventing immediate unity among the diffused atoms; and these atoms are represented as different each from each. Difference is their character – their essentiality – just as no-difference was the essentiality of their course. When we say, then, that an attempt to bring any two of these atoms together would induce an effort on the part of the repulsive influence to prevent the contact, we may as well use the strictly convertible sentence that an attempt to bring together any two differences will result in a development of electricity. All existing bodies, of course, are composed of these atoms in proximate contact, and are therefore to be considered as mere assemblages of more or fewer differences; and the resistance made by the repulsive spirit on bringing together any two such assemblages would be in the ratio of the two sums of the differences in each – an expression which, when reduced, is equivalent to this: the amount of electricity developed on the approximation of two bodies is proportional with the difference between the respective sums of the atoms of which the bodies are composed. That no two bodies are absolutely alike is a simple corollary from all that has been here said. Electricity, therefore, existing always, is *developed* whenever any bodies, but *manifested* only when bodies of appreciable difference are brought into approximation.

To electricity – so, for the present, continuing to call it – we may not be wrong in referring the various physical appearances of light, heat, and magnetism; but far less shall we be liable to err in attributing to this strictly spiritual principle the more important phenomena of vitality, consciousness, and thought. On this topic, however, I need pause here merely to suggest that these phenomena, whether observed generally or in detail, seem to proceed at least in the ratio of the heterogeneous.

Discarding now the two equivocal terms, 'gravitation' and 'electricity', let us adopt the more definite expressions, 'attraction' and 'repulsion'. The former is the body, the latter the soul; the one is the material, the other the spiritual principle of the universe. No other principles exist. All phenomena are referable to one or to the other, or to both combined. So rigorously is this the case, so thoroughly demonstrable is it that attraction and repulsion are the sole properties through which we perceive the universe – in other words, by which matter is manifested to mind – that, for all merely argumentative purposes, we are fully justified in assuming that matter exists only as attraction and repulsion, that attraction and repulsion *are* matter; there being no conceivable case in which we may not employ the term 'matter' and the terms 'attraction' and 'repulsion', taken together, as equivalent, and therefore convertible, expressions in logic.

I said, just now, that what I have described as the tendency of the diffused atoms to return into their original unity would be understood as the principle of the Newtonian law of gravity, and, in fact, there can be but little difficulty in such an understanding if we look at the Newtonian gravity in a merely general view, as a force impelling matter to seek matter, that is to say when we pay no attention to the known *modus operandi* of the Newtonian force. The general coincidence satisfies us; but, on looking closely, we see in detail much that appears *incoincident*, and much in regard to which no coincidence, at least, is established. For example, the Newtonian gravity, when we think of it in certain moods, does not seem to be a tendency to oneness at all, but rather a tendency of all bodies in all directions – a phrase apparently expressive of a tendency to diffusion. Here, then, is an *incoincidence*. Again, when we reflect on the mathematical law governing the Newtonian tendency, we see clearly that no coincidence has been made good, in respect of the *modus operandi*, at least, between gravity as known to exist and that seemingly simple and direct tendency which I have assumed.

In fact, I have attained a point at which it will be advisable to strengthen my position by reversing my processes. So far, we have gone on a priori, from an abstract consideration of simplicity as that quality most likely to have characterised the original action of God. Let us now see whether the established facts of the Newtonian gravitation may not afford us, a posteriori, some legitimate inductions.

What does the Newtonian law declare? That all bodies attract each other with forces proportional with their quantities of matter, and inversely proportional with the squares of their distances. Purposely, I have given, in the first place, the vulgar version of the law, and I confess that in this, as in most other vulgar versions of great truths, we find little of a suggestive character. Let us now adopt a more philosophical phraseology: every atom, of every body, attracts every other atom, both of its own and of every other body, with a force which varies inversely as the squares of the distances between the attracting and attracted atom. Here, indeed, a flood of suggestion bursts upon the mind.

But let us see distinctly what it was that Newton *proved* – according to the grossly irrational definitions of *proof* prescribed by the metaphysical schools. He was forced to content himself with showing how thoroughly the motions of an imaginary universe, composed of attracting and attracted atoms obedient to the law he announced, coincide with those of the actually existing universe so far as it comes under our observation. This was the amount of his demonstration; that is to say, this was the amount of it, according to the conventional cant of the 'philosophies'. His successors added proof multiplied by proof – such proof as a sound intellect admits – but the demonstration of the law itself, persist the metaphysicians, had not been strengthened in any degree. 'Ocular, physical proof,' however, of attraction here upon Earth in accordance with the Newtonian theory, was at length, much to the satisfaction of some intellectual grovellers, afforded. This proof arose collaterally and incidentally (as nearly all important truths have arisen) out of an attempt to ascertain the mean density of the Earth. In the famous Maskelyne, Cavendish and Bailly experiments for this purpose, the attraction of the mass of a mountain[2] was seen, felt, measured, and found to be mathematically consistent with the theory of the British astronomer.

But in spite of this confirmation of that which needed none, in spite of the so-called corroboration of the 'theory' by the so-called 'ocular and physical proof', in spite of the character of this corroboration, the ideas which even really philosophical men cannot help imbibing of Gravity – and, especially, the ideas of it which ordinary men get and contentedly maintain – are seen to have been derived, for the most part, from a consideration of the principle as they find it developed merely in the planet upon which they stand.

Now, to what does so partial a consideration tend – to what species of error does it give rise? On the Earth we see and feel only that gravity impels all bodies towards the centre of the Earth. No man in the common walks of life could be made to see or feel anything else – could be made to perceive that anything, anywhere, has a perpetual, gravitating tendency in any other direction than to the centre of the Earth. Yet (with an exception hereafter to be specified) it is a fact that every earthly thing (not to speak now of every heavenly thing) has a tendency not only to the Earth's centre, but in every conceivable direction besides.

Now, although the philosophic cannot be said to err with the vulgar in this matter, they nevertheless permit themselves to be influenced, without knowing it, by the sentiment of the vulgar idea. 'Although the pagan fables are not believed,' says Bryant, in his very erudite *Mythology*, 'yet we forget ourselves continually, and make inferences from them as from existing realities.' I mean to assert that the merely sensitive perception of gravity, as we experience it on Earth, beguiles mankind into the fancy of concentralisation or speciality respecting it – has been continually biasing towards this fancy even the mightiest intellects – perpetually, although imperceptibly, leading them away from the real characteristics of the principle; thus preventing them, up to this date, from ever getting a glimpse of that vital truth which lies in a diametrically opposite direction – behind the principle's essential characteristics – those, not of concentralisation or speciality, but of universality and diffusion. This 'vital truth' is unity as the source of the phenomenon.

Let me now repeat the definition of gravity: every atom, of every body, attracts every other atom, both of its own and of every other body, with a force which varies inversely as the squares of the distances of the attracting and attracted atom.

Here let the reader pause with me for a moment in contemplation of the miraculous, of the ineffable, of the altogether unimaginable complexity of relation involved in the fact that each atom attracts every other atom; involved merely in this fact of the attraction, without reference to the law or mode in which the attraction is manifested; involved merely in the fact that each atom attracts every other atom at all, in a wilderness of atoms so numerous that those which go to the composition of a cannon-ball exceed, probably, in mere point of number, all the stars which go to the constitution of the universe.

Had we discovered, simply, that each atom tends to some one point, a favourite with all, we should still have fallen upon a discovery which, in itself, would have sufficed to overwhelm the mind; but what is it that we are actually called on to comprehend? That each atom attracts, sympathises with the most delicate movements of every other atom, and with each and with all at the same time, and forever, and according to a determinate law of which the complexity, even considered by itself solely, is utterly beyond the grasp of the imagination. If I propose to ascertain the influence of one mote in a sunbeam on its neighbouring mote, I cannot accomplish my purpose without first counting and weighing all the atoms in the universe, and defining the precise positions of all at one particular moment. If I venture to displace, by even the billionth part of an inch, the microscopic speck of dust which lies now upon the point of my finger, what is the character of that act upon which I have adventured? I have done a deed which shakes the Moon in her path, which causes the Sun to be no longer the Sun, and which alters forever the destiny of the multitudinous myriads of stars that roll and glow in the majestic presence of their creator.

These ideas – conceptions such as these – unthoughtlike thoughts – soul-reveries rather than conclusions or even considerations of the intellect – ideas, I repeat, such as these, are such as we can alone hope profitably to entertain in any effort at grasping the great principle, attraction.

But now, with such ideas, with such a vision of the marvellous complexity of attraction fairly in his mind, let any person competent of thought on such topics as these, set himself to the task of imagining a principle for the phenomena observed – a condition from which they sprang.

Does not so evident a brotherhood among the atoms point to a common parentage? Does not a sympathy so omniprevalent, so ineradicable, and so thoroughly irrespective, suggest a common paternity as its source? Does not one extreme impel the reason to the other? Does not the infinitude of division refer to the utterness of individuality? Does not the entireness of the complex hint at the perfection of the simple? It is not that the atoms, as we see them, are divided, or that they are complex in their relations, but that they are inconceivably divided and unutterably complex. It is the extremeness of the conditions to which I now allude, rather than to the conditions themselves. In a word, is it not because the atoms were, at some remote epoch of time, even more than together – is it not because originally, and therefore normally, they were one – that now, in all circumstances, at all points, in all directions, by all modes of approach, in all relations and through all conditions, they struggle back to this absolutely, this irrelatively, this unconditionally one?

Some person may here demand: 'Why, since it is to the one that the atoms struggle back, do we not find and define attraction as 'merely a general tendency to a centre'? Why, in special, do not your atoms, the atoms which you describe as having been radiated from a centre, proceed at once, rectilinearly, back to the central point of their origin?'

I reply that they do, as will be distinctly shown, but that the cause of their so doing is quite irrespective of the centre as such. They all tend rectilinearly towards a centre, because of the sphericity with which they have been radiated into space. Each atom, forming one of a generally uniform globe of atoms, finds more atoms in the direction of the centre, of course, than in any other, and in that direction, therefore, is impelled – but is not thus impelled because the centre is the point of its origin. It is not to any point that the atoms are allied. It is not any locality, either in the concrete or in the abstract, to which I suppose them bound. Nothing like location was conceived as their origin. Their source lies in the principle, unity. This is their lost parent. This they seek always – immediately – in all directions – wherever it is even partially to be found, thus appeasing, in some measure, the ineradicable tendency, while on the way to its absolute satisfaction in the end. It follows from all this that any principle which shall be adequate to account for the law, or *modus operandi*, of the attractive force in general, will account for this law in particular; that is to say, any principle which will show why the atoms should tend to their general centre of radiation with forces inversely proportional with the squares of the distances will be admitted as satisfactorily accounting, at the same time, for the tendency, according to the same law, of these atoms each to each. For the tendency to the centre is merely the tendency each to each, and not any tendency to a centre as such. Thus it will be seen, also, that the establishment of my propositions would involve no necessity of modification in the terms of the Newtonian definition of gravity which declares that each atom attracts each other atom and so forth, and declares this merely; but (always under the supposition that what I propose be, in the end, admitted) it seems clear that some error might occasionally be avoided in the future processes of science were a more ample phraseology adopted. For instance: 'Each atom tends to every other atom, etc., with a force, etc.; the general result being a tendency of all, with a similar force, to a general centre.'

The reversal of our processes has thus brought us to an identical result; but while in the one process intuition was the starting-point, in the other it was the goal. In commencing the former journey I could only say that with an irresistible intuition I felt simplicity to have been the characteristic of the original action of God. In ending the latter I can only declare that with an irresistible intuition I perceive unity to have been the source of the observed phenomena of the Newtonian gravity. Thus, according to the schools, I prove nothing. So be it. I design but to suggest, and to convince through the suggestion. I am proudly aware that there exist many of the most profound and cautiously discriminative intellects which cannot help being abundantly content with my suggestions. To these intellects, as to my own, there is no mathematical demonstration which could bring the least additional true proof of the great truth which I have advanced, the truth of original unity as the source, as the principle, of the universal phenomena. For my part I am not sure that I speak and see – I am not so sure that my heart beats and that my soul lives; of the rising of tomorrow's sun – a probability that as yet lies in the future. I do not pretend to be one thousandth part as sure as I am of the irretrievably bygone fact that all things and all thoughts of things, with all their ineffable multiplicity of relation, sprang at once into being from the primordial and irrelative one.

Referring to the Newtonian gravity, Dr Nichol, the eloquent author of *The Architecture of the Heavens*, says: 'In truth we have no reason to suppose this great law, as now revealed, to be the ultimate or simplest, and therefore the universal and all-comprehensive, form of a great ordinance. The mode in which its intensity diminishes with the element of distance has not the aspect of an ultimate principle; which always assumes the simplicity and self-evidence of those axioms which constitute the basis of geometry.'

Now, it is quite true that 'ultimate principles', in the common understanding of the words, always assume the simplicity of geometrical axioms – (as for 'self-evidence', there is no such thing) – but these principles are clearly not 'ultimate'. In other terms, what we are in the habit of calling principles are not principles, properly speaking, since there can be but one principle, the volition of God. We have no right to assume, then, from what we observe in rules that we choose foolishly to name 'principles', anything at all in respect to the characteristics of a principle proper. The 'ultimate principles' of which Dr Nichol speaks as having geometrical simplicity may and do have this geometrical turn, as being part and parcel of a vast geometrical system, and thus a system of simplicity itself; in which, nevertheless, the truly ultimate principle is, as we know, the consummation of the complex – that is to say, of the unintelligible – for is it not the spiritual capacity of God?

I quoted Dr Nichol's remark, however, not so much to question its philosophy, as by way of calling attention to the fact that while all men have admitted *some* principle as existing behind the law of gravity, no attempt has been yet made to point out what this principle in particular *is* – if we except, perhaps, occasional fantastic efforts at referring it to magnetism or mesmerism or Swedenborgianism or transcendentalism or some other equally delicious *ism* of the same species and invariably patronised by one and the same species of people. The great mind of Newton, while boldly grasping the law itself, shrank from the principle of the law. The more fluent and comprehensive at least, if not the more patient and profound, sagacity of Laplace had not the courage to attack it. But hesitation on the part of these two astronomers is, perhaps, not so very difficult to understand. They, as well as all the first class of mathematicians, were mathematicians solely; their intellect at least had a firmly pronounced mathematico-physical tone. What lay not distinctly within the domain of physics, or of mathematics, seemed to them either non-entity or shadow. Nevertheless, we may well wonder that Leibnitz, who was a marked exception to the general rule in these respects, and whose mental temperament was a singular admixture of the mathematical with the physico-metaphysical, did not at once investigate and establish the point at issue. Either Newton or Laplace, seeking a principle and discovering none physical, would have rested contentedly in the conclusion that there was absolutely none. But it is almost impossible to fancy, of Leibnitz, that, having exhausted in his search the physical dominions, he would not have stepped at once, boldly and hopefully, amid his old familiar haunts in the kingdom of metaphysics. Here, indeed, it is clear that he must have adventured in search of the treasure. That he did not find it after all, was, perhaps, because his fairy guide, imagination, was not sufficiently well-grown, or well-educated, to direct him aright.

I observed, just now, that in fact there had been certain vague attempts at referring gravity to some very uncertain *isms*. These attempts, however, although considered bold, and justly so considered, looked no further than to the generality – the merest generality – of the Newtonian law. Its *modus operandi* has never, to my knowledge, been approached in the way of an effort at explanation. It is, therefore, with no unwarranted fear of being taken for a madman at the outset, and before I can bring my propositions fairly to the eye of those who alone are competent to decide on them, that I here declare the *modus operandi* of the law of gravity to be an exceedingly simple and perfectly explicable thing, that is to say, when we make our advances towards it in just gradations and in the true direction, when we regard it from the proper point of view.

Whether we reach the idea of absolute unity as the source of all things from a consideration of simplicity as the most probable characteristic of the original action of God, whether we arrive at it from an inspection of the universality of relation in the gravitating phenomena, or whether we attain it as a result of the mutual corroboration afforded by both processes, still, the idea itself, if entertained at all, is entertained in inseparable connection with another idea – that of the condition of the universe of stars as we now perceive it, that is to say a condition of immeasurable diffusion through space. Now, a connection between these two ideas, unity and diffusion, cannot be established unless through the entertainment of a third idea, that of radiation. Absolute unity being taken as a centre, then the existing universe of stars is the result of radiation from that centre.

Now, the laws of radiation are known. They are part and parcel of the sphere. They belong to the class of indisputable geometrical properties. We say of them, 'they are true, they are evident.' To demand why they are true would be to demand why the axioms are true upon which their demonstration is based. Nothing is demonstrable, strictly speaking; but if anything be, then the properties, the laws in question, are demonstrated.

But these laws – what do they declare? Radiation – how? – by what steps does it proceed outwardly from a centre?

From a luminous centre, light issues by radiation; and the quantities of light received upon any given plane, supposed to be shifting its position so as to be now nearer the centre and now further from it, will be diminished in the same proportion as the squares of the distances of the plane from the luminous body are increased, and will be increased in the same proportion as these squares are diminished.

The expression of the law may be thus generalised: the number of light-particles (or, if the phrase be preferred, the number of light-impressions) received upon the shifting plane will be inversely proportional with the squares of the distances of the plane. Generalising yet again, we may say that the diffusion, the scattering, the irradiation, in a word, is directly proportional with the squares of the distances.

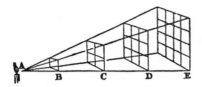

For example: at the distance B from the luminous centre A, a certain number of particles are so diffused as to occupy the surface B.

Then at double the distance, that is to say at C, they will be so much further diffused as to occupy four such surfaces; at treble the distance, or at D, they will be so much further separated as to occupy nine such surfaces; while, at quadruple the distance, or at E, they will have become so scattered as to spread themselves over sixteen such surfaces – and so on forever.

In saying, generally, that the radiation proceeds in direct proportion with the squares of the distances, we use the term radiation to express the degree of the diffusion as we proceed outwardly from the centre. Conversing the idea, and employing the word 'concentralisation' to express the degree of the drawing together as we come back toward the centre from an outward position, we may say that concentralisation proceeds inversely as the squares of the distances. In other words, we have reached the conclusion that, on the hypothesis that matter was originally radiated from a centre, and is now returning to it, the concentralisation, in the return, proceeds exactly as we know the force of gravitation to proceed.

Now here, if we could be permitted to assume that concentralisation exactly represents the force of the tendency to the centre – that the one is exactly proportional with the other, and that the two proceed together – we should have shown all that is required. The sole difficulty existing, then, is to establish a direct proportion between 'concentralisation' and the *force* of concentralisation; and this is done, of course, if we establish such proportion between 'radiation' and the *force* of radiation.

A very slight inspection of the heavens assures us that the stars have a certain general uniformity, equability, or equidistance, of distribution through that region of space in which, collectively, and in a roughly globular form, they are situated; this species of very general, rather than absolute, equability being in full keeping with my deduction of inequidistance, within certain limits, among the originally diffused atoms, as a corollary from the evident design of infinite complexity of relation out of irrelation. I started, it will be remembered, with the idea of a generally uniform but particularly *un*uniform distribution of the atoms – an idea, I repeat, which an inspection of the stars, as they exist, confirms.

But even in the merely general equability of distribution, as regards the atoms, there appears a difficulty which, no doubt, has already suggested itself to those among my readers who have borne in mind that I suppose this equability of distribution effected through radiation from a centre. The very first glance at the idea, radiation, forces us to the entertainment of the hitherto unseparated and seemingly inseparable idea of agglomeration about a centre, with dispersion as we recede from it – the idea, in a word, of *inequability* of distribution in respect to the matter irradiated.

Now, I have elsewhere observed[3] that it is by just such difficulties as the one now in question – such peculiarities, such roughnesses, such protuberances above the plane of the ordinary – that reason feels her way, if at all, in her search for the true. By the difficulty, the 'peculiarity' now presented, I leap at once to the secret; a secret which I might never have attained but for the peculiarity and the inferences which, in its mere character of peculiarity, it affords me.

The process of thought, at this point, may be thus roughly sketched: I say to myself, 'Unity, as I have explained it, is a truth: I feel it. Diffusion is a truth: I see it. Radiation, by which alone these two truths are reconciled, is a consequent truth: I perceive it. Equability of diffusion, first deduced a priori and then corroborated by the inspection of phenomena, is also a truth: I fully admit it. So far all is clear around me; there are no clouds behind which the secret – the great secret of the gravitating *modus operandi* – can possibly lie hidden. But this secret lies hereabouts, most assuredly; and were there but a cloud in view, I should be driven to suspicion of that cloud.' And now, just as I say this, there actually comes a cloud into view. This cloud is the seeming impossibility of reconciling my truth, *radiation*, with my truth, *equability of diffusion*.

I say now: 'Behind this seeming impossibility is to be found what I desire.' I do not say '*real* impossibility', for invincible faith in my truths assures me that it is a mere difficulty, after all. But I go on to say with unflinching confidence that, *when* this difficulty shall be solved, we shall find, wrapped up in the process of solution, the key to the secret at which we aim. Moreover, I feel that we shall discover but one possible solution of the difficulty; this for the reason that, were there two, one would be supererogatory – would be fruitless – would be empty – would contain no key – since no duplicate key can be needed to any secret of Nature.

And now, let us see … Our usual notions of radiation, in fact *all* our distinct notions of it, are caught merely from the process as we see it exemplified in light. Here there is a continuous outpouring of ray streams, and with a force which we have at least no right to suppose varies at all. Now, in any such radiation as this, continuous and of unvarying force, the regions nearer the centre must inevitably be always more crowded with the radiated matter than the regions more remote. But I have assumed no such radiation as this. I assumed no continuous radiation, and for the simple reason that such an assumption would have involved, first, the necessity of entertaining a conception which I have shown no man can entertain, and which (as I will more fully explain hereafter) all observation of the firmament refutes – the conception of the absolute infinity of the universe of stars; and would have involved, secondly, the impossibility of understanding a reaction – that is, gravitation – as existing now, since, while an act is continued, no reaction of course can take place. My assumption, then, or rather my inevitable deduction from just premises, was that of a determinate radiation – one finally discontinued.

Let me now describe the sole possible mode in which it is conceivable that matter could have been diffused through space so as to fulfil the conditions at once of radiation and of generally equable distribution.

For convenience of illustration, let us imagine in the first place a hollow sphere of glass, or of anything else, occupying the space throughout which the universal matter is to be thus equally diffused, by means of radiation, from the absolute, irrelative, unconditional particle placed in the centre of the sphere.

Now, a certain exertion of the diffusive power (presumed to be the divine volition) – in other words, a certain force whose measure is the quantity of matter, that is to say, the number of atoms, emitted – emits by radiation this certain number of atoms, forcing them in all directions outwardly from the centre, their proximity to each other diminishing as they proceed, until, finally, they are distributed loosely over the interior surface of the sphere.

When these atoms have attained this position, or while proceeding to attain it, a second and inferior exercise of the same force – or a second and inferior force of the same character – emits in the same manner, that is to say by radiation as before, a second stratum of atoms which proceeds to deposit itself upon the first; the number of atoms, in this case as in the former, being of course the measure of the force which emitted them: in other words, the force being precisely adapted to the purpose it effects – the force, and the number of atoms sent out by the force, being directly proportional.

When this second stratum has reached its destined position, or while approaching it, a third still inferior exertion of the force, or a third inferior force of a similar character – the number of atoms emitted being in all cases the measure of the force – proceeds to deposit a third stratum upon the second; and so on, until these concentric strata, growing gradually less and less, come down at length to the central point; and the diffusive matter, simultaneously with the diffusive force, is exhausted.[4]

We have now the sphere filled, through means of radiation, with atoms equably diffused. The two necessary conditions – those of radiation and of equable diffusion – are satisfied; and by the sole process in which the possibility of their simultaneous satisfaction is conceivable. For this reason, I confidently expect to find, lurking in the present condition of the atoms as distributed throughout the sphere, the secret of which I am in search – the all-important principle of the *modus operandi* of the Newtonian law. Let us examine, then, the actual condition of the atoms.

They lie in a series of concentric strata. They are equably diffused throughout the sphere.

The atoms being equably distributed, the greater the superficial extent of any of these concentric strata, or spheres, the more atoms will lie upon it. In other words, the number of atoms lying upon the surface of any one of the concentric spheres is directly proportional with the extent of that surface.

But in any series of concentric spheres the surfaces are directly proportional with the squares of the distances from the centre.[5] Therefore the number of atoms in any stratum is directly proportional with the square of that stratum's distance from the centre. But the number of atoms in any stratum is the measure of the force which emitted that stratum, that is to say, is directly proportional with the force. Therefore the force which radiated any stratum is directly proportional with the square of that stratum's distance from the centre. Or, generally, the force of the irradiation has been directly proportional with the squares of the distances; or particularly, the force by which any individual atom was sent to its position in the sphere was directly proportional with the square of that atom's distance, while in that position, from the centre of the sphere.

Now, reaction, as far as we know anything of it, is action conversed. The general principle of gravity being in the first place understood as the reaction of an act, as the expression of a desire on the part of matter, while existing in a state of diffusion, to return into the unity whence it was diffused; and in the second place the mind being called on to determine the character of the desire, the manner in which it would naturally be manifested. In other words, being called on to conceive a probable law, or *modus operandi*, for the return, the mind could not well help arriving at the conclusion that this law of return would be precisely the converse of the law of departure. That such would be the case, anyone at least would be abundantly justified in taking for granted until such time as some person should suggest something like a plausible reason why it should not be the case – until such a period as a law of return shall be imagined which the intellect can consider as preferable.

Matter, then, radiated into space with a force varying as the squares of the distances, might a priori be supposed to return towards its centre of radiation with a force varying inversely as the squares of the distances. And I have already shown[6] that any principle which will explain why the atoms should tend, according to any law, to the general centre must be admitted as satisfactorily explaining, at the same time, why according to the same law they should tend each to each. For, in fact, the tendency to the general centre is not to a centre as such, but because of its being a point in tending towards which each atom tends most directly to its real and essential centre, unity – the absolute and final union of all.

The consideration here involved presents to my own mind no embarrassment whatever, but this fact does not blind me to the possibility of its being obscure to those who may have been less in the habit of dealing with abstractions; and, upon the whole, it may be as well to look at the matter from one or two other points of view.

The absolute, irrelative particle, primarily created by the volition of God, must have been in a condition of positive normality, or rightfulness, for wrongfulness implies relation. Right is positive; wrong is negative, merely the negation of right, as cold is the negation of heat, darkness of light. That a thing may be wrong, it is necessary that there be some other thing in relation to which it is wrong – some condition which it fails to satisfy, some law which it violates, some being whom it aggrieves. If there be no such being, law, or condition, in respect to which the thing is wrong – and, still more specially, if no beings, laws, or conditions exist at all – then the thing cannot be wrong and consequently must be right.

Any deviation from normality involves a tendency to return to it. A difference from the normal – from the right, from the just – can be understood as effected only by the overcoming of a difficulty. And, if the force which overcomes the difficulty be not infinitely continued, the ineradicable tendency to return will at length be permitted to act for its own satisfaction. On withdrawal of the force, the tendency acts. This is the principle of reaction as the inevitable consequence of finite action. Employing a phraseology of which the seeming affectation will be pardoned for its expressiveness, we may say that reaction is the return from the condition of as it is and ought not to be into the condition of as it was, originally, and therefore ought to be. And let me add here that the absolute force of reaction would no doubt be always found in direct proportion with the reality – the truth, the absoluteness – of the originality, if ever it were possible to measure this latter. And, consequently, the greatest of all conceivable reactions must be that manifested in the tendency which we now discuss – the tendency to return into the absolutely original, into the supremely primitive. Gravity, then, must be the strongest of forces – an idea reached a priori, and abundantly confirmed by induction. What use I make of the idea will be seen in the sequel.

The atoms, now, having been diffused from their normal condition of unity, seek to return to – what? Not to any particular point, certainly; for it is clear that if on the diffusion the whole universe of matter had been projected, collectively, to a distance from the point of radiation, the atomic tendency to the general centre of the sphere would not have been disturbed in the least; the atoms would not have sought the point in absolute space from which they were originally impelled. It is merely the condition, and not the point or locality at which this condition took its rise, that these atoms seek to re-establish; it is merely that condition which is their normality that they desire. 'But they seek a centre,' it will be said, 'and a centre is a point.' True, but they seek this point not in its character of point – (for, were the whole sphere moved from its position, they would seek equally the centre, and the centre then would be a new point) – but because it so happens on account of the form in which they collectively exist (that of the sphere) that only *through* the point in question – the sphere's centre – they can attain their true object, unity. In the direction of the centre each atom perceives more atoms than in any other direction. Each atom is impelled towards the centre because along the straight line joining it and the centre and passing on to the circumference beyond there lie a greater number of atoms than along any other straight line – a greater number of objects that seek it, the individual atom – a greater number of tendencies to unity – a greater number of satisfactions for its own tendency to unity – in a word, because in the direction of the centre lies the utmost possibility of satisfaction, generally, for its own individual appetite. To be brief, the condition unity is all that is really sought; and if the atoms seem to seek the centre of the sphere, it is only impliedly – through implication – because such centre happens to imply, to include, or to involve, the only essential centre, unity. But on account of this implication or involution, there is no possibility of practically separating the tendency to unity in the abstract from the tendency to the concrete centre. Thus the tendency of the atoms to the general centre *is*, to all practical intents and for all logical purposes, the tendency each to each; and the tendency each to each *is* the tendency to the centre; and the one tendency may be assumed as the other; whatever will apply to the one must be thoroughly applicable to the other; and, in conclusion, whatever principle will satisfactorily explain the one, cannot be questioned as an explanation of the other.

In looking carefully around me for rational objection to what I have advanced, I am able to discover nothing. But of that class of objections usually urged by the doubters for doubt's sake, I very readily perceive three, and proceed to dispose of them in order.

It may be said, first: 'That the proof that the force of radiation (in the case described) is directly proportional to the squares of the distances depends upon an unwarranted assumption – that of the number of atoms in each stratum being the measure of the force with which they are emitted.'

I reply not only that I am warranted in such assumption but that I should be utterly unwarranted in any other. What I assume is simply that an effect is the measure of its cause; that every exercise of the divine will will be proportional with that which demands the exertion; that the means of omnipotence, or of omniscience, will be exactly adapted to its purposes. Neither can a deficiency nor an excess of cause bring to pass any effect. Had the force which radiated any stratum to its position been either more or less than was needed for the purpose – that is to say, not directly proportional with the purpose – then to its position that stratum could not have been radiated. Had the force which, with a view to general equability of distribution, emitted the proper number of atoms for each stratum been not directly proportional with the number, then the number would not have been the number demanded for the equable distribution.

The second supposable objection is somewhat better entitled to an answer.

It is an admitted principle in dynamics that every body, on receiving an impulse or disposition to move will move onward in a straight line in the direction imparted by the impelling force until deflected or stopped by some other force. How then, it may be asked, is my first or external stratum of atoms to be understood as discontinuing their movement at the surface of the imaginary glass sphere when no second force, of more than an imaginary character, appears to account for the discontinuance?

I reply that the objection, in this case, actually does arise out of 'an unwarranted assumption' – on the part of the objector – the assumption of a principle, in dynamics, at an epoch when no 'principles' in *anything* exist. I use the word 'principle', of course, in the objector's understanding of the word.

'In the beginning' we can admit, indeed we can comprehend, but one first cause, the truly ultimate principle – the volition of God. The primary act – that of radiation from unity – must have been independent of all that which the world now calls 'principle', because all that we so designate is but a consequence of the reaction of that primary act. I say 'primary' act, for the creation of the absolute material particle is more properly to be regarded as a conception than as an '*act*' in the ordinary meaning of the term. Thus we must regard the primary act as an act for the establishment of what we now call 'principles'. But this primary act itself is to be considered as continuous volition. The thought of God is to be understood as originating the diffusion – as proceeding with it, as regulating it and finally as being withdrawn from it upon its completion. *Then* commences reaction, and through reaction, 'principle', as we employ the word. It will be advisable, however, to limit the application of this word to the two immediate results of the discontinuance of the divine volition – that is, to the two agents, attraction and repulsion. Every other natural agent depends, either more or less immediately, upon these two, and therefore would be more conveniently designated as sub-principle.

It may be objected thirdly that, in general, the peculiar mode of distribution which I have suggested for the atoms is 'a hypothesis and nothing more'.

Now, I am aware that the word 'hypothesis' is a ponderous sledgehammer, grasped immediately, if not lifted, by all very diminutive thinkers on the first appearance of any proposition wearing, in any particular, the garb of a theory. But 'hypothesis' cannot be wielded here to any good purpose, even by those who succeed in lifting it, little men or great.

I maintain, first, that only in the mode described is it conceivable that matter could have been diffused so as to fulfil at once the conditions of radiation and of generally equable distribution. I maintain, secondly, that these conditions themselves have been imposed upon me, as necessities, in a train of ratiocination as rigorously logical as that which establishes any demonstration in Euclid. And I maintain, thirdly, that even if the charge of 'hypothesis' were as fully sustained as it is, in fact, unsustained and untenable, still the validity and indisputability of my result would not, even in the slightest particular, be disturbed.

To explain: the Newtonian gravity – a law of Nature; a law whose existence as such no one out of Bedlam questions; a law whose admission as such enables us to account for nine-tenths of the universal phenomena; a law which, merely because it does so enable us to account for these phenomena, we are perfectly willing, without reference to any other considerations, to admit, and cannot help admitting, as a law; a law, nevertheless, of which neither the principle nor the *modus operandi* of the principle has ever yet been traced by the human analysis; a law, in short, which neither in its detail nor in its generality has been found susceptible of explanation at all – is at length seen to be at every point thoroughly explicable, provided we only yield our assent to – what? To a hypothesis? Why, if a hypothesis – if the merest hypothesis; if a hypothesis for whose assumption, as in the case of that pure hypothesis the Newtonian law itself, no shadow of a-priori reason could be assigned; if a hypothesis even so absolute as all this implies would enable us to perceive a principle for the Newtonian law; would enable us to understand as satisfied conditions so miraculously, so ineffably complex and seemingly irreconcilable as those involved in the relations of which gravity tells us – what rational being could so expose his fatuity as to call even this absolute hypothesis a hypothesis any longer; unless, indeed, he were to persist in so calling it, with the understanding that he did so simply for the sake of consistency in words?

But what is the true state of our present case? What is the fact? Not only that it is not a hypothesis which we are required to adopt in order to admit the principle at issue explained, but that it is a logical conclusion which we are requested *not* to adopt if we can avoid it, which we are simply invited to deny if we can; a conclusion of so accurate a logicality that to dispute it would be the effort; to doubt its validity, beyond our power – a conclusion from which we see no mode of escape, turn as we will; a result which confronts us either at the end of an inductive journey from the phenomena of the very law discussed, or at the close of a deductive career from the most rigorously simple of all conceivable assumptions – the assumption, in a word, of simplicity itself.

And if here it be urged that although my starting-point is, as I assert, the assumption of absolute simplicity, yet simplicity, considered merely in itself, is no axiom, and that only deductions from axioms are indisputable, it is thus that I reply: every other science than logic is the science of certain concrete relations. Arithmetic, for example, is the science of the relations of number; geometry, of the relations of form; mathematics in general, of the relations of quantity in general – of whatever can be increased or diminished. Logic, however, is the science of relation in the abstract, of absolute relation, of relation considered solely in itself. An axiom in any particular science other than logic is, thus, merely a proposition announcing certain concrete relations which seem to be too obvious for dispute – as when we say, for instance, that the whole is greater than its part; and, thus again, the principle of the logical axiom – in other words, of an axiom in the abstract – is simply obviousness of relation. Now, it is clear not only that what is obvious to one mind may not be obvious to another, but that what is obvious to one mind at one epoch, may be anything but obvious at another epoch to the same mind. It is clear, moreover, that what today is obvious even to the majority of mankind, or to the majority of the best intellects of mankind, may tomorrow be, to either majority, more or less obvious, or in no respect obvious at all. It is seen, then, that the axiomatic principle itself is susceptible of variation, and of course that axioms are susceptible of similar change. Being mutable, the 'truths' which grow out of them are necessarily mutable too; or, in other words, are never to be positively depended on as truths at all – since truth and immutability are one.

It will now be readily understood that no axiomatic idea, no idea founded in the fluctuating principle, obviousness of relation, can possibly be so secure, so reliable a basis for any structure erected by the reason, as that idea (whatever it is, wherever we can find it, indeed if it be practicable to find it anywhere) which is irrelative altogether; which not only presents to the understanding no obviousness of relation, either greater or less, to be considered, but subjects the intellect not in the slightest degree to the necessity of even looking at any relation at all. If such an idea be not what we too heedlessly term 'an axiom', it is at least preferable as a logical basis to any axiom ever propounded, or to all imaginable axioms combined; and such precisely is the idea with which my deductive process, so thoroughly corroborated by induction, commences. My 'particle proper' is but absolute relation.

To sum up what has been advanced: as a starting-point I have taken it for granted, simply, that the beginning had nothing behind it or before it, that it was a beginning in fact, that it was a beginning and nothing different from a beginning; in short, that this beginning was that which it was. If this be a 'mere assumption', then a 'mere assumption' let it be.

To conclude this branch of the subject: I am fully warranted in announcing that the law which we call gravity exists on account of matter's having been radiated, at its origin, atomically, into a limited sphere of space[7], from one, individual, unconditional, irrelative, and absolute particle proper, by the sole process in which it was possible to satisfy, at the same time, the two conditions, radiation and equable distribution throughout the sphere; that is to say, by a force varying in direct proportion with the squares of the distances between the radiated atoms, respectively, and the particular centre of radiation.

I have already given my reasons for presuming matter to have been diffused by a determinate rather than by a continuous or infinitely continued force. Supposing a continuous force, we should be unable, in the first place, to comprehend a reaction at all; and we should be required, in the second place, to entertain the impossible conception of an infinite extension of matter. Not to dwell upon the impossibility of the conception, the infinite extension of matter is an idea which, if not positively disproved, is at least not in any respect warranted by telescopic observation of the stars – a point to be explained more fully hereafter; and this empirical reason for believing in the original finity of matter is unempirically confirmed. For example, admitting for the moment the possibility of understanding space as filled with the radiated atoms – that is to say, admitting, as well as we can, for argument's sake, that the succession of the radiated atoms had absolutely no end – then it is clear that even when the volition of God had been withdrawn from them, and thus the tendency to return into unity permitted (abstractly) to be satisfied, this permission would have been nugatory and invalid, practically valueless and of no effect whatever. No reaction could have taken place; no movement towards unity could have been made; no law of gravity could have been obtained.

To explain: grant the abstract tendency of any one atom to any one other as the inevitable result of diffusion from the normal unity; or, what is the same thing, admit any given atom as proposing to move in any given direction, it is clear that since there is an infinity of atoms on all sides of the atom proposing to move, it never can actually move towards the satisfaction of its tendency in the direction given on account of a precisely equal and counterbalancing tendency in the direction diametrically opposite. In other words, exactly as many tendencies to unity are behind the hesitating atom as before it; for it is mere folly to say that one infinite line is longer or shorter than another infinite line, or that one infinite number is greater or less than another number that is infinite. Thus the atom in question must remain stationary for ever. Under the impossible circumstances which we have been merely endeavouring to conceive for argument's sake, there could have been no aggregation of matter – no stars – no worlds – nothing but a perpetually atomic and inconsequential universe. In fact, view it as we will, the whole idea of unlimited matter is not only untenable, but impossible and preposterous.

With the understanding of a sphere of atoms, however, we

perceive at once a satisfiable tendency to union. The general result of the tendency each to each being a tendency of all to the centre, the general process of condensation, or approximation, commences immediately by a common and simultaneous movement on withdrawal of the divine volition; the individual approximations, or coalescences of atom with atom, being subject to almost infinite variations of time, degree, and condition, on account of the excessive multiplicity of relation, arising from the differences of form assumed as characterising the atoms at the moment of their quitting the particle proper; as well as from the subsequent particular inequidistance, each from each.

What I wish to impress upon the reader is the certainty of there arising, at once (on withdrawal of the diffusive force or divine volition), out of the condition of the atoms as described, at innumerable points throughout the universal sphere, innumerable agglomerations characterised by innumerable specific differences of form, size, essential nature, and distance each from each. The development of repulsion (electricity) must have commenced, of course, with the very earliest particular efforts at unity, and must have proceeded constantly in the ratio of coalescence – that is to say, in that of condensation, or, again, of heterogeneity. Thus the two principles proper, attraction and repulsion – the material and the spiritual – accompany each other, in the strictest fellowship, for ever. Thus the body and the soul walk hand in hand.

If now, in fancy, we select any one of the agglomerations considered as in their primary stages throughout the universal sphere, and suppose this incipient agglomeration to be taking place at that point where the centre of our Sun exists – or rather where it did exist originally for the Sun is perpetually shifting his position – we shall find ourselves met, and borne onward for a time at least, by the most magnificent of theories, by the nebular cosmogony of Laplace, although 'cosmogony' is far too comprehensive a term for what he really discusses – which is the constitution of our solar system alone – of one among the myriad of similar systems which make up the universe of stars.

Confining himself to an obviously limited region – that of our solar system with its comparatively immediate vicinity – and merely assuming, that is to say, assuming without any basis whatever, much of what I have been just endeavouring to place upon a more stable basis than assumption; assuming, for example, matter as diffused (without pretending to account for the diffusion) throughout, and somewhat beyond, the space occupied by our system, diffused in a state of heterogeneous nebulosity and obedient to that omniprevalent law of gravity at whose principle he ventured to make no guess; assuming all this (which is quite true, although he had no logical right to its assumption), Laplace has shown, dynamically and mathematically, that the results in such case necessarily ensuing are those, and those alone, which we find manifested in the actually existing condition of the system itself.

To explain: let us conceive that particular agglomeration of which we have just spoken – the one at the point designated by our Sun's centre – to have so far proceeded that a vast quantity of nebulous matter has here assumed a roughly globular form; its centre being, of course, coincident with what is now, or rather was originally, the centre of our Sun; and its surface extending out beyond the orbit of Neptune, the most remote of our planets; in other words, let us suppose the diameter of this rough sphere to be some six thousand million miles. For ages, this mass of matter has been undergoing condensation, until at length it has become reduced into the bulk we imagine, having proceeded gradually, of course, from its atomic and imperceptible state into what we understand of appreciable nebulosity.

Now, the condition of this mass implies a rotation about an imaginary axis; a rotation which, commencing with the absolute incipiency of the aggregation, has been ever since acquiring velocity. The very first two atoms which met, approaching each other from points not diametrically opposite, would, in rushing partially past each other, form a nucleus for the rotary movement described. How this would increase in velocity is readily seen. The two atoms are joined by others. An aggregation is formed.

The mass continues to rotate while condensing. But any atom at the circumference has, of course, a more rapid motion than one nearer the centre. The outer atom, however, with its superior velocity, approaches the centre, carrying this superior velocity with it as it goes. Thus every atom, proceeding inwardly, and finally attaching itself to the condensed centre, adds something to the original velocity of that centre – that is to say, increases the rotary movement of the mass.

Let us now suppose this mass so far condensed that it occupies precisely the space circumscribed by the orbit of Neptune, and that the velocity with which the surface of the mass moves, in the general rotation, is precisely that velocity with which Neptune now revolves about the Sun. At this epoch, then, we are to understand that the constantly increasing centrifugal force, having got the better of the non-increasing centripetal, loosened and separated the exterior and least condensed stratum, or a few of the exterior and least condensed strata, at the equator of the sphere where the tangential velocity predominated, so that these strata formed about the main body an independent ring encircling the equatorial regions; just as the exterior portion thrown off by excessive velocity of rotation from a grindstone would form a ring about the grindstone, but for the solidity of the superficial material. Were this caoutchouc[8], or anything similar in consistency, precisely the phenomenon I describe would be presented.

The ring thus whirled from the nebulous mass revolved, of course, as a separate ring with just that velocity with which, while the surface of the mass, it rotated. In the meantime, condensation still proceeding, the interval between the discharged ring and the main body continued to increase until the former was left at a vast distance from the latter.

Now, admitting the ring to have possessed, by some seemingly accidental arrangement of its heterogeneous materials, a constitution nearly uniform, then this ring, as such, would never have ceased revolving about its primary. But, as might have been anticipated, there appears to have been enough irregularity in the disposition of the materials to make them cluster about centres of superior solidity; and thus the annular form was destroyed.[9]

No doubt the band was soon broken up into several portions, and one of these portions, predominating in mass, absorbed the others into itself; the whole settling, spherically, into a planet. That this latter, as a planet, continued the revolutionary movement which characterised it while a ring, is sufficiently clear; and that it took upon itself, also, an additional movement in its new condition of sphere, is readily explained. The ring being understood as yet unbroken, we see that its exterior, while the whole revolves about the parent body, moves more rapidly than its interior. When the rupture occurred, then, some portion in each fragment must have been moving with greater velocity than the others. The superior movement prevailing must have whirled each fragment round, that is to say, have caused it to rotate; and the direction of the rotation must, of course, have been the direction of the revolution whence it arose. All the fragments, having become subject to the rotation described, must, in coalescing, have imparted it to the one planet constituted by their coalescence. This planet was Neptune. Its material continuing to undergo condensation, and the centrifugal force, generated in its rotation, getting at length the better of the centripetal, as before in the case of the parent orb, a ring was whirled also from the equatorial surface of this planet. This ring, having been uniform in its constitution, was broken up, and its several fragments, being absorbed by the most massive, were collectively spherified into a moon. Subsequently, the operation was repeated, and a second moon was the result. We thus account for the planet Neptune with the two satellites which accompany him.[10]

In throwing off a ring from its equator, the Sun re-established that equilibrium between its centripetal and centrifugal forces which had been disturbed in the process of condensation. But, as this condensation still proceeded, the equilibrium was again immediately disturbed through the increase of rotation. By the time the mass had so far shrunk that it occupied a spherical space just that circumscribed by the orbit of Uranus, we are to understand that the centrifugal force had so far obtained the ascendancy that new relief was needed. A second equatorial band was consequently thrown off which proving un-uniform was broken up, as before in the case of Neptune; the fragments settling into the planet Uranus – the velocity of whose actual revolution about the Sun indicates, of course, the rotary speed of that Sun's equatorial surface at the moment of the separation. Uranus, adopting a rotation from the collective rotations of the fragments composing it, as previously explained, now threw off ring after ring; each of which, becoming broken up, settled into a moon – three moons, at different epochs, having been formed in this manner by the rupture and general spherification of as many distinct un-uniform rings.

By the time the Sun had shrunk until it occupied a space just that circumscribed by the orbit of Saturn, the balance, we are to suppose, between its centripetal and centrifugal forces had again become so far disturbed through increase of rotary velocity, the result of condensation, that a third effort at equilibrium became necessary; and an annular band was therefore whirled off, as twice before, which on rupture through un-uniformity became consolidated into the planet Saturn. This latter threw off, in the first place, seven un-uniform bands, which on rupture were spherified respectively into as many moons. But subsequently it appears to have discharged, at three distinct but not very distant epochs, three rings whose equability of constitution was, by apparent accident, so considerable as to present no occasion for their rupture; thus they continue to revolve as rings. I use the phrase 'apparent accident' for of accident in the ordinary sense there was, of course, nothing – the term is properly applied only to the result of indistinguishable or not immediately traceable law.

Shrinking still further, until it occupied just the space circumscribed by the orbit of Jupiter, the Sun now found need of further effort to restore the counterbalance of its two forces, continually disarranged in the still continued increase of rotation. Jupiter, accordingly, was now thrown off, passing from the annular to the planetary condition; and, on attaining this latter,

55

threw off in its turn, at four different epochs, four rings which finally resolved themselves into so many moons.

Still shrinking, until its sphere occupied just the space defined by the orbit of the asteroids, the Sun now discarded a ring which appears to have had nine centres of superior solidity, and on breaking up to have separated into nine fragments, no one of which so far predominated in mass as to absorb the others.[11] All therefore, as distinct although comparatively small planets, proceeded to revolve in orbits whose distances, each from each, may be considered as in some degree the measure of the force which drove them asunder; all the orbits, nevertheless, being so closely coincident as to admit of our calling them one, in view of the other planetary orbits.

Continuing to shrink, the Sun, on becoming so small as just to fill the orbit of Mars, now discharged this planet – of course by the process repeatedly described. Since he had no moon, however, Mars could have thrown off no ring. In fact, an epoch had now arrived in the career of the parent body, the centre of the system. The decrease of its nebulosity – which is the increase of its density, and which again is the decrease of its condensation, out of which latter arose the constant disturbance of equilibrium – must, by this period, have attained a point at which the efforts for restoration would have been more and more ineffectual just in proportion as they were less frequently needed. Thus the processes of which we have been speaking would everywhere show signs of exhaustion – in the planets first, and secondly in the original mass. We must not fall into the error of supposing the decrease of interval observed among the planets as we approach the Sun to be in any respect indicative of an increase of frequency in the periods at which they were discarded. Exactly the converse is to be understood. The longest interval of time must have occurred between the discharges of the two interior; the shortest, between those of the two exterior planets. The decrease of the interval of space is, nevertheless, the measure of the density, and thus inversely of the condensation, of the Sun throughout the processes detailed.

Having shrunk, however, so far as to fill only the orbit of our Earth, the parent sphere whirled from itself still one other body – the Earth – in a condition so nebulous as to admit of this body's discarding, in its turn, yet another, which is our Moon; but here terminated the lunar formations.

Finally, subsiding to the orbits first of Venus and then of Mercury, the Sun discarded these two interior planets; neither of which has given birth to any moon.

Thus from his original bulk, or to speak more accurately, from the condition in which we first considered him – from a partially spherified nebular mass, certainly much more than five thousand, six hundred million miles in diameter – the great central orb and origin of our solar-planetary-lunar system has gradually descended, by condensation, in obedience to the law of gravity to a globe only eight hundred eighty-two thousand miles in diameter; but it by no means follows either that its condensation is yet complete, or that it may not still possess the capacity of whirling from itself another planet.

I have here given – in outline, of course, but still with all the detail necessary for distinctness – a view of the nebular theory as its author himself conceived it. From whatever point we regard it, we shall find it beautifully true. It is by far too beautiful, indeed, not to possess truth as its essentiality – and here I am very profoundly serious in what I say. In the revolution of the satellites of Uranus, there does appear something seemingly inconsistent with the assumptions of Laplace; but that one inconsistency can invalidate a theory constructed from a million of intricate consistencies is a fancy fit only for the fantastic. In prophesying, confidently, that the apparent anomaly to which I refer will, sooner or later, be found one of the strongest possible corro-borations of the general hypothesis, I pretend to no special spirit of divination. It is a matter which the only difficulty seems *not* to foresee.[12]

The bodies whirled off in the processes described would exchange, it has been seen, the superficial rotation of the orbs whence they originated for a revolution of equal velocity about

57

these orbs as distant centres; and the revolution thus engendered must proceed, so long as the centripetal force, or that with which the discarded body gravitates toward its parent, is neither greater nor less than that by which it was discarded; that is, than the centrifugal, or, far more properly, than the tangential, velocity. From the unity, however, of the origin of these two forces we might have expected to find them as they are found – the one accurately counterbalancing the other. It has been shown, indeed, that the act of whirling-off is, in every case, merely an act for the preservation of the counterbalance.

After referring, however, the centripetal force to the omni-prevalent law of gravity, it has been the fashion with astronomical treatises to seek beyond the limits of mere Nature – that is to say, of secondary cause – a solution of the phenomenon of tangential velocity. This latter they attribute directly to a first cause – to God. The force which carries a stellar body around its primary they assert to have originated in an impulse given immediately by the finger – this is the childish phraseology employed – by the finger of deity itself. In this view, the planets, fully formed, are conceived to have been hurled from the divine hand to a position in the vicinity of the suns with an impetus mathematically adapted to the masses, or attractive capacities, of the suns themselves. An idea so grossly unphilosophical, although so supinely adopted, could have arisen only from the difficulty of otherwise accounting for the absolutely accurate adaptation, each to each, of two forces so seemingly independent, one of the other, as are the gravitating and tangential. But it should be remembered that for a long time the coincidence between the moon's rotation and her sidereal revolution – two matters seemingly far more independent than those now considered – was looked upon as positively miraculous; and there was a strong disposition, even among astronomers, to attribute the marvel to the direct and continual agency of God, who in this case it was said had found it necessary to interpose specially among His general laws a set of subsidiary regulations for the purpose of forever concealing from mortal eyes the glories, or perhaps the horrors, of the other side of the Moon – of that mysterious hemisphere which has always avoided, and must perpetually avoid, the telescopic scrutiny of mankind. The advance of science, however, soon demonstrated what to the philosophical instinct needed no demonstration: that the one movement is but a portion – something more, even, than a consequence – of the other.

For my part, I have no patience with fantasies at once so timorous, so idle, and so awkward. They belong to the veriest cowardice of thought. That Nature and the God of Nature are distinct, no thinking being can long doubt. By the former we imply merely the laws of the latter. But with the very idea of God, omnipotent, omniscient, we entertain also the idea of the infallibility of his laws. With Him there being neither past nor future – with Him all being *now* – do we not insult Him in supposing His laws so contrived as not to provide for every possible contingency? Or rather, what idea can we have of any possible contingency, except that it is at once a result and a manifestation of His laws? He who, divesting himself of prejudice, shall have the rare courage to think absolutely for himself, cannot fail to arrive in the end at the condensation of laws into Law – cannot fail of reaching the conclusion that each law of Nature is dependent at all points upon all other laws, and that all are but consequences of one primary exercise of the divine volition. Such is the principle of the cosmogony which, with all necessary deference, I here venture to suggest and to maintain.

In this view, it will be seen that, dismissing as frivolous and even impious, the fancy of the tangential force having been imparted to the planets immediately by 'the finger of God', I consider this force as originating in the rotation of the stars; this rotation as brought about by the in-rushing of the primary atoms towards their respective centres of aggregation; this in-rushing as the consequence of the law of gravity; this law as but the mode in which is necessarily manifested the tendency of the atoms to return into imparticularity; this tendency as but the inevitable reaction of the first and most sublime of acts – that act by which a

God, self-existing and alone existing, became all things at once through dint of His volition, while all things were thus constituted a portion of God.

The radical assumptions of this discourse suggest to me, and in fact imply, certain important modifications of the nebular theory as given by Laplace. The efforts of the repulsive power I have considered as made for the purpose of preventing contact among the atoms, and thus as made in the ratio of the approach to contact – that is to say, in the ratio of condensation.[13] In other words, electricity, with its involute phenomena, heat, light, and magnetism, is to be understood as proceeding as condensation proceeds, and, of course, inversely as density proceeds or the cessation to condense. Thus the Sun, in the process of its consolidation, must soon, in developing repulsion, have become excessively heated – incandescent. And we can perceive how the operation of discarding its rings must have been materially assisted by the slight encrustation of its surface consequent on cooling. Any common experiment shows us how readily a crust, of the character suggested, is separated through heterogeneity from the interior mass. But, on every successive rejection of the crust, the new surface would appear incandescent as before; and the period at which it would again become so far encrusted as to be readily loosened and discharged may well be imagined as exactly coincident with that at which a new effort would be needed, by the whole mass, to restore the equilibrium of its two forces, disarranged through condensation. In other words, by the time the electric influence (repulsion) has prepared the surface for rejection, we are to understand that the gravitating influence (attraction) is precisely ready to reject it. Here, then, as everywhere, the body and the soul walk hand in hand.

These ideas are empirically confirmed at all points. Since condensation can never, in any body, be considered as absolutely at an end, we are warranted in anticipating that whenever we have an opportunity of testing the matter we shall find indications of resident luminosity in all the stellar bodies – moons and planets as well as suns. That our Moon is strongly self-luminous we see at her every total eclipse, when, if not so, she would disappear. On the dark part of the satellite, too, during her phases, we often observe flashes like our own auroras; and that these latter, with our various other so-called electrical phenomena, without reference to any more steady radiance, must give our Earth a certain appearance of luminosity to an inhabitant of the Moon, is quite evident. In fact, we should regard all the phenomena referred to as mere manifestations, in different moods and degrees, of the Earth's feebly continued condensation.

If my views are tenable, we should be prepared to find the newer planets – that is to say, those nearer the Sun – more luminous than those older and more remote. And the extreme brilliancy of Venus (on whose dark portions, during her phases, the auroras are frequently visible) does not seem to be altogether accounted for by her mere proximity to the central orb. She is no doubt vividly self-luminous, although less so than Mercury: while the luminosity of Neptune may be comparatively nothing.

Admitting what I have urged, it is clear that from the moment of the Sun's discarding a ring there must be a continuous diminution both of his heat and light on account of the continuous encrustation of his surface; and that a period would arrive – the period immediately previous to a new discharge – when a very material decrease of both light and heat must become apparent. Now, we know that tokens of such changes are distinctly recognisable. On the Melville Islands, to adduce merely one out of a hundred examples, we find traces of ultra-tropical vegetation – of plants that never could have flourished without immensely more light and heat than are at present afforded by our Sun to any portion of the surface of the Earth. Is such vegetation referable to an epoch immediately subsequent to the whirling-off of Venus? At this epoch must have occurred to us our greatest access of solar influence; and, in fact, this influence must then have attained its maximum, leaving out of view, of course, the period when the Earth itself was discarded, the period of its mere organisation.

Again, we know that there exist non-luminous suns – that is to say, suns whose existence we determine through the movements of others, but whose luminosity is not sufficient to impress us. Are these suns invisible merely on account of the length of time elapsed since their discharge of a planet? And yet again, may we not, at least in certain cases, account for the sudden appearances of suns where none had been previously suspected by the hypothesis that, having rolled with encrusted surfaces throughout the few thousand years of our astronomical history, each of these suns in whirling off a new secondary has at length been enabled to display the glories of its still incandescent interior? To the well-ascertained fact of the proportional increase of heat as we descend into the Earth, I need of course do nothing more than refer; it comes in the strongest possible corroboration of all that I have said on the topic now at issue.

In speaking not long ago of the repulsive or electrical influence, I remarked that 'the important phenomena of vitality, consciousness, and thought, whether we observe them generally or in detail, seem to proceed at least in the ratio of the heterogeneous.'[14] I mentioned, too, that I would recur to the suggestion, and this is the proper point at which to do so. Looking at the matter, first in detail, we perceive that not merely the manifestation of vitality, but its importance, consequences, and elevation of character, keep pace very closely with the heterogeneity, or complexity, of the animal structure. Looking at the question, now, in its generality, and referring to the first movements of the atoms towards mass-constitution, we find that heterogeneousness, brought about directly through condensation, is proportional with it forever. We thus reach the proposition that the importance of the development of the terrestrial vitality proceeds equably with the terrestrial condensation.

Now, this is in precise accordance with what we know of the succession of animals on the Earth. As it has proceeded in its condensation, superior and still superior races have appeared. Is it impossible that the successive geological revolutions which have attended, at least, if not immediately caused, these successive elevations of vitalistic character – is it improbable that these revolutions have themselves been produced by the successive planetary discharges from the Sun; in other words, by the successive variations in the solar influence on the Earth? Were this idea tenable, we should not be unwarranted in the fancy that the discharge of yet a new planet, interior to Mercury, may give rise to yet a new modification of the terrestrial surface – a modification from which may spring a race both materially and spiritually superior to Man. These thoughts impress me with all the force of truth, but I throw them out, of course, merely in their obvious character of suggestion.

The nebular theory of Laplace has lately received far more confirmation than it needed, at the hands of the philosopher Comte. These two have thus together shown – not, to be sure, that matter at any period actually existed as described in a state of nebular diffusion – but that, admitting it so to have existed throughout the space and much beyond the space now occupied by our solar system, and to have commenced a movement towards a centre, it must gradually have assumed the various forms and motions which are now seen, in that system, to obtain. A demonstration such as this – a dynamic and mathematical demonstration, as far as demonstrations can be, unquestionable and unquestioned, unless, indeed, by that unprofitable and disreputable tribe, the professional questioners, the mere madmen who deny the Newtonian law of gravity on which the results of the French mathematicians are based – a demonstration, I say, such as this, would to most intellects be conclusive, and I confess that it is so to mine, of the validity of the nebular hypothesis upon which the demonstration depends.

That the demonstration does not prove the hypothesis, according to the common understanding of the word 'proof', I admit, of course. To show that certain existing results, that certain established facts, may be, even mathematically, accounted for by the assumption of a certain hypothesis, is by no means to establish the hypothesis itself. In other words, to show that, certain data being given, a certain existing result might, or even must, have ensued will fail to prove that this result *did* ensue *from the data* until such time as it shall be also shown that there are, and can be, no other data from which the result in question might equally have ensued. But, in the case now discussed, although all must admit the deficiency of what we are in the habit of terming 'proof', still there are many intellects, and those of the loftiest order, to which no proof could bring one iota of additional conviction. Without going into details which might impinge upon the cloud-land of metaphysics, I may as well here observe that the force of conviction in cases such as this will always, with the right thinking, be proportional to the amount of complexity intervening between the hypothesis and the result. To be less abstract: the greatness of the complexity found existing among cosmic conditions, by rendering great in the same proportion the difficulty of accounting for all these conditions, at once strengthens also in the same proportion our faith in that hypothesis which does, in such manner, satisfactorily account for them. And as no complexity can well be conceived greater than that of the astronomical conditions, so no conviction can be stronger – to my mind at least – than that with which I am impressed by a hypothesis that not only reconciles these conditions with mathematical accuracy, and reduces them into a consistent and intelligible whole, but is, at the same time, the sole hypothesis by means of which the human intellect has been ever enabled to account for them at all.

A most unfounded opinion has been latterly current in gossiping and even in scientific circles – the opinion that the so-called nebular cosmogony has been overthrown. This fancy has arisen from the report of late observations made, among what hitherto have been termed the 'nebulae', through the large telescope of Cincinnati, and the world-renowned instrument of Lord Rosse. Certain spots in the firmament which presented, even to the most powerful of the old telescopes, the appearance of nebulosity or haze had been regarded for a long time as confirming the theory of Laplace. They were looked upon as stars in that very process of condensation which I have been attempting to describe. Thus it was supposed that we 'had ocular evidence' – an evidence, by the way, which has always been found very questionable – of the truth of the hypothesis. And, although certain telescopic improvements every now and then enabled us to perceive that a spot, here and there, which we had been classing among the nebulae, was in fact but a cluster of stars deriving its nebular character only from its immensity of distance, still it was thought that no doubt could exist as to the actual nebulosity of numerous other masses, the strongholds of the nebulists, bidding defiance to every effort at segregation. Of these latter the most interesting was the great 'nebula' in the constellation Orion; but this, with innumerable other mis-called 'nebulae', when viewed through the magnificent modern telescopes, has become resolved into a simple collection of stars. Now, this fact has been very generally understood as conclusive against the nebular hypothesis of Laplace. And, on announcement of the discoveries in question, the most enthu-siastic defender and most eloquent populariser of the theory, Dr Nichol, went so far as to 'admit the necessity of abandoning' an idea which had formed the material of his most praiseworthy book[15].

Many of my readers will no doubt be inclined to say that the result of these new investigations has at least a strong tendency to overthrow the hypothesis; while some of them, more thoughtful, will suggest that, although the theory is by no means disproved through the segregation of the particular 'nebulae' alluded to, still a failure to segregate them, with such telescopes, might well have been understood as a triumphant corroboration of the theory; and this latter class will be surprised, perhaps, to hear me say that even with them I disagree. If the propositions of this discourse have been comprehended, it will be seen that in my view a failure to segregate the 'nebulae' would have tended to the refutation, rather than to the confirmation, of the nebular hypothesis.

Let me explain: the Newtonian law of gravity we may, of course, assume as demonstrated. This law, it will be remembered, I have referred to the reaction of the first divine act – to the reaction of an exercise of the divine volition temporarily overcoming a difficulty. This difficulty is that of forcing the normal into the abnormal – of impelling that whose originality, and therefore whose rightful condition, was one, to take upon itself the wrongful condition of many. It is only by conceiving this difficulty as temporarily overcome that we can comprehend a reaction. There could have been no reaction had the act been infinitely continued. So long as the act lasted, no reaction of course could commence; in other words, no gravitation could take place, for we have considered the one as but the manifestation of the other. But gravitation has taken place; therefore the act of creation has ceased. And gravitation has long ago taken place; therefore the act of creation has long ago ceased. We can no more expect, then, to observe the primary processes of creation, and to these primary processes the condition of nebulosity has already been explained to belong.

Through what we know of the propagation of light, we have direct proof that the more remote of the stars have existed, under the forms in which we now see them, for an inconceivable number of years. So far back at least, then, as the period when these stars underwent condensation must have been the epoch at which the mass-constitutive processes began. That we may conceive these processes, then, as still going on in the case of certain 'nebulae', while in all other cases we find them thoroughly at an end, we are forced into assumptions for which we have really no basis whatever; we have to thrust in, again, upon the revolting reason, the blasphemous idea, of special interposition; we have to suppose that in the particular instances of these 'nebulae' an unerring God found it necessary to introduce certain supplementary regulations – certain improvements of the general law – certain retouchings and emendations, in a word, which had the effect of deferring the completion of these individual stars for centuries of centuries beyond the era during which all the other stellar bodies had time, not only to be fully constituted, but to grow hoary with an unspeakable old age.

Of course, it will be immediately objected that, since the light by which we recognise the nebulae now must be merely that which left their surfaces a vast number of years ago, the processes at present observed, or supposed to be observed, are in fact not processes now actually going on, but the phantoms of processes completed long in the past – just as I maintain all these mass-constitutive processes must have been.

To this I reply that neither is the now-observed condition of the condensed stars their actual condition, but a condition completed long in the past, so that my argument drawn from the *relative* condition of the stars and the 'nebulae' is in no manner disturbed. Moreover, those who maintain the existence of nebulae do not refer the nebulosity to extreme distance; they declare it a real and not merely a perspective nebulosity. That we may conceive, indeed, a nebular mass as visible at all, we must conceive it as very near us in comparison with the condensed stars brought into view by the modern telescopes. In maintaining the appearances in question, then, to be really nebulous, we maintain their comparative vicinity to our point of view. Thus, their condition, as we see them now, must be referred to an epoch far less remote than that to which we may refer the now-observed condition of at least the majority of the stars. In a word, should astronomy ever demonstrate a 'nebula' in the sense at present intended, I should consider the nebular cosmogony – not, indeed, as corroborated by the demonstration – but as thereby irretrievably overthrown.

By way, however, of rendering unto Caesar no more than the things that are Caesar's, let me here remark that the assumption of the hypothesis which led him to so glorious a result seems to have been suggested to Laplace in great measure by a misconception – by the very misconception of which we have just been speaking – by the generally prevalent misunderstanding of the character of the nebulae, so misnamed. These he supposed to be, in reality, what their designation implies. The fact is, this great man had, very properly, an inferior faith in his own merely perceptive powers. In respect, therefore, to the actual existence of nebulae, an existence so confidently maintained by his telescopic contemporaries, he depended less upon what he saw than upon what he heard.

It will be seen that the only valid objections to his theory are those made to its hypothesis as such – to what suggested it, not to what it suggests – to its propositions rather than to its results. His most unwarranted assumption was that of giving the atoms a movement towards a centre, in the very face of his evident understanding that these atoms, in unlimited succession, extended throughout the universal space. I have already shown that, under such circumstances, there could have occurred no movement at all; and Laplace consequently assumed one on no more philosophical a ground than that something of the kind was necessary for the establishment of what he intended to establish.

His original idea seems to have been a compound of the true Epicurean atoms with the false nebulae of his contemporaries; and thus his theory presents us with the singular anomaly of absolute truth deduced, as a mathematical result, from a hybrid datum of ancient imagination intertangled with modern inacumen. Laplace's real strength lay, in fact, in an almost miraculous mathematical instinct. On this he relied, and in no instance did it fail or deceive him. In the case of the nebular cosmogony, it led him, blindfolded, through a labyrinth of error into one of the most luminous and stupendous temples of truth.

Let us now fancy – merely fancy – for the moment, that the ring first thrown off by the Sun – that is to say, the ring whose breaking-up constituted Neptune – did not, in fact, break up until the throwing-off of the ring out of which Uranus arose; that this latter ring, again, remained perfect until the discharge of that out of which sprang Saturn; that this latter, again, remained entire until the discharge of that from which originated Jupiter, and so on. Let us imagine, in a word, that no dissolution occurred among the rings until the final rejection of that which gave birth to Mercury. We thus paint to the eye of the mind a series of coexistent concentric circles, and looking as well at them as at the processes by which, according to Laplace's hypothesis, they were constructed, we perceive at once a very singular analogy with the atomic strata and the process of the original radiation as I have described it. Is it impossible that on measuring the forces respectively by which each successive planetary circle was thrown off – that is to say, on measuring the successive excesses of rotation over gravitation which occasioned the successive discharges – we should find the analogy in question more decidedly confirmed? Is it improbable that we should discover these forces to have varied, as in the original radiation, proportionally with the squares of the distances?

Our solar system, consisting in chief of one sun, with seventeen planets certainly, and possibly a few more, revolving about it at various distances, and attended by seventeen moons assuredly, but very probably by several others, is now to be considered as an *example* of the innumerable agglomerations which proceeded to take place throughout the universal sphere of atoms on withdrawal of the divine volition. I mean to say that our solar system is to be understood as affording a generic instance of these agglomerations, or, more correctly, of the ulterior conditions at which they arrived. If we keep our attention fixed on the idea of the utmost possible relation as the omnipotent design, and on the precautions taken to accomplish it through difference of form among the original atoms and particular inequidistance, we shall find it impossible to suppose for a moment that even any two of the incipient agglomerations reached precisely the same result in the end. We shall rather be inclined to think that no two stellar bodies in the universe – whether suns, planets, or moons – are particularly, while all are generally, similar. Still less, then, can we imagine any two assemblages of such bodies – any two 'systems' – as having more than a general resemblance.[16] Our telescopes, at this point, thoroughly confirm our deductions. Taking our own solar system, then, as merely a loose or general type of all, we have so far proceeded in our subject as to survey the universe of stars under the aspect of a spherical space, throughout which, dispersed with merely general equability, exist a number of but generally similar systems.

Let us now, expanding our conceptions, look upon each of

these systems as in itself an atom, which in fact it is, when we consider it as but one of the countless myriads of systems which constitute the universe. Regarding all, then, as but colossal atoms, each with the same ineradicable tendency to unity which characterises the actual atoms of which it consists, we enter at once a new order of aggregations. The smaller systems, in the vicinity of a larger one, would inevitably be drawn into still closer vicinity. A thousand would assemble here; a million there – perhaps here, again, even a billion – leaving, thus, immeasurable vacancies in space. And if, now, it be demanded why, in the case of these systems, of these merely Titanic atoms, I speak simply of an 'assemblage' and not, as in the case of the actual atoms, of a more or less consolidated agglomeration; if it be asked, for instance, why I do not carry what I suggest to its legitimate conclusion, and describe at once these assemblages of system-atoms as rushing to consolidation in spheres, as each becoming condensed into one magnificent sun, my reply is that *mellonta tauta*[17] – I am but pausing, for a moment, on the awful threshold of the future. For the present, calling these assemblages 'clusters', we see them in the incipient stages of their consolidation. Their absolute consolidation is to come.

We have now reached a point from which we behold the universe of stars as a spherical space, interspersed unequably with clusters. It will be noticed that I here prefer the adverb 'unequably' to the phrase 'with a merely general equability', employed before. It is evident, in fact, that the equability of distribution will diminish in the ratio of the agglomerative processes – that is to say, as the things distributed diminish in number. Thus the increase of inequability – an increase which must continue until, sooner or later, an epoch will arrive at which the largest agglomeration will absorb all the others – should be viewed as simply a corroborative indication of the tendency to one.

And here, at length, it seems proper to enquire whether the ascertained facts of astronomy confirm the general arrangement which I have thus, deductively, assigned to the Heavens.

Thoroughly, they do. Telescopic observation, guided by the laws of perspective, enables us to understand that the perceptible universe exists as a roughly spherical cluster of clusters, irregularly disposed.

The 'clusters' of which this universal 'cluster of clusters' consists are merely what we have been in the practice of designating 'nebulae' – and, of these 'nebulae', one is of paramount interest to mankind. I allude to the galaxy, or Milky Way. This interests us, first and most obviously, on account of its great superiority in apparent size, not only to any one other cluster in the firmament, but to all the other clusters taken together. The largest of these latter occupies a mere point, comparatively, and is distinctly seen only with the aid of a telescope. The galaxy sweeps throughout the heaven, and is brilliantly visible to the naked eye. But it interests man chiefly, although less immediately, on account of its being his home; the home of the Earth on which he exists; the home of the Sun about which this Earth revolves; the home of that 'system' of orbs of which the Sun is the centre and primary, the Earth one of seventeen secondaries or planets, the Moon one of seventeen tertiaries or satellites. The galaxy, let me repeat, is but one of the clusters which I have been describing; but one of the miscalled 'nebulae' revealed to us – by the telescope alone, sometimes – as faint hazy spots in various quarters of the sky. We have no reason to suppose the Milky Way really more extensive than the least of these 'nebulae'. Its vast superiority in size is but an apparent superiority arising from our position in regard to it – that is to say, from our position in its midst. However strange the assertion may at first appear to those unversed in astronomy, still the astronomer himself has no hesitation in asserting that we are in the midst of that inconceivable host of stars – of suns – of systems – which constitute the galaxy. Moreover, not only have we, not only has our Sun a right to claim the galaxy as its own special cluster, but, with slight reservation, it may be said that all the distinctly visible stars of the firmament, all the stars visible to the naked eye, have equally a right to claim it as their own.

There has been a great deal of misconception in respect to the shape of the galaxy, which, in nearly all our astronomical treatises, is said to resemble that of a capital Y. The cluster in question has, in reality, a certain general, very general resemblance to the planet Saturn with its encompassing triple ring. Instead of the solid orb of that planet, however, we must picture to ourselves a lenticular star-island, or collection of stars; our Sun lying eccentrically – near the shore of the island – on that side of it which is nearest the constellation of the Cross and furthest from that of Cassiopeia. The surrounding ring, where it approaches our position, has in it a longitudinal gash, which does in fact cause the ring, in our vicinity, to assume loosely the appearance of a capital Y.

We must not fall into the error, however, of conceiving the somewhat indefinite girdle as at all remote, comparatively speaking, from the also indefinite lenticular cluster which it surrounds. And thus, for mere purpose of explanation, we may speak of our Sun as actually situated at that point of the Y where its three component lines unite; and, conceiving this letter to be of a certain solidity – of a certain thickness, very trivial in comparison with its length – we may even speak of our position as in the middle of this thickness. Fancying ourselves thus placed, we shall no longer find difficulty in accounting for the phenomena presented, which are perspective altogether. When we look upward or downward – that is to say, when we cast our eyes in the direction of the letter's thickness – we look through fewer stars than when we cast them in the direction of its length, or along either of the three component lines. Of course, in the former case, the stars appear scattered; in the latter, crowded. To reverse this explanation: an inhabitant of the Earth, when looking, as we commonly express ourselves, *at* the galaxy, is then beholding it in some of the directions of its length – is looking *along* the lines of the Y; but when, looking out into the general heaven, he turns his eyes *from* the galaxy, he is then surveying it in the direction of the letter's thickness; and on this account the stars seem to him scattered, while in fact they are as close together, on an average, as in the mass of the cluster. No consideration could be better adapted to convey an idea of this cluster's stupendous extent.

If, with a telescope of high space-penetrating power, we carefully inspect the firmament, we shall become aware of a belt of clusters – of what we have hitherto called 'nebulae' – a band of varying breadth stretching from horizon to horizon at right angles to the general course of the Milky Way. This band is the ultimate cluster of clusters. This belt is the universe of stars. Our galaxy is but one, and perhaps one of the most inconsiderable, of the clusters which go to the constitution of this ultimate, universal belt or band. The appearance of this cluster of clusters, to our eyes, as a belt or band, is altogether a perspective phenomenon of the same character as that which causes us to behold our own individual and roughly spherical cluster, the galaxy, under guise also of a belt, traversing the heavens at right angles to the universal one. The shape of the all-inclusive cluster is, of course, generally that of each individual cluster which it includes. Just as the scattered stars which, on looking *from* the galaxy, we see in the general sky, are in fact but a portion of that galaxy itself, and as closely intermingled with it as any of the telescopic points in what seems the densest portion of its mass, so are the scattered 'nebulae' which, on casting our eyes *from* the universal belt, we perceive at all points of the firmament. So, I say, are these scattered 'nebulae' to be understood as only perspectively scattered, and as but a portion of the one supreme and universal sphere.

No astronomical fallacy is more untenable, and none has been more pertinaciously adhered to, than that of the absolute 'illimitation' of the universe of stars. The reasons for limitation, as I have already assigned them, a priori, seem to me unanswerable; but, not to speak of these, observation assures us that there is, in numerous directions around us, certainly, if not in all, a positive limit – or, at the very least, affords us no basis whatever for thinking otherwise. Were the succession of stars endless, then the background of the sky would present us a uniform luminosity, like that displayed by the galaxy – since there could be absolutely no point, in all that background, at which would not exist a star.

The only mode, therefore, in which under such a state of affairs we could comprehend the voids which our telescopes find in innumerable directions would be by supposing the distance of the invisible background so immense that no ray from it has yet been able to reach us at all. That this may be so, who shall venture to deny? I maintain, simply, that we have not even the shadow of a reason for believing that it is so.

When speaking of the vulgar propensity to regard all bodies on the Earth as tending merely to the Earth's centre, I observed that, 'with certain exceptions to be specified hereafter, every body on the Earth tended not only to the Earth's centre, but in every conceivable direction besides.'[18] The 'exceptions' refer to those frequent gaps in the heavens where our utmost scrutiny can detect not only no stellar bodies, but no indications of their existence; where yawning chasms, blacker than Erebus, seem to afford us glimpses through the boundary walls of the universe of stars into the illimitable universe of vacancy beyond. Now, as any body existing on the Earth chances to pass, either through its own movement or the Earth's, into a line with any one of these voids or cosmic abysses, it clearly is no longer attracted in the direction of that void, and for the moment, consequently, is 'heavier' than at any period, either after or before. Independently of the consideration of these voids, however, and looking only at the generally unequable distribution of the stars, we see that the absolute tendency of bodies on the Earth to the Earth's centre is in a state of perpetual variation.

We comprehend, then, the insulation of our universe. We perceive the isolation of that, of all that which we grasp with the senses. We know that there exists one cluster of clusters – a collection around which, on all sides, extend the immeasurable wildernesses of a space to all human perception untenanted. But because upon the confines of this universe of stars we are compelled to pause, through want of further evidence from the senses, is it right to conclude that in fact there *is* no material point beyond that which we have thus been permitted to attain? Have we, or have we not, an analogical right to the inference that this perceptible universe, that this cluster of clusters, is but one of a series of clusters of clusters, the rest of which are invisible through distance, through the diffusion of their light being so excessive ere it reaches us as not to produce upon our retinas a light-impression, or from there being no such emanation as light at all, in those unspeakably distant worlds, or lastly from the mere interval being so vast that the electric tidings of their presence in space have not yet – through the lapsing myriads of years – been enabled to traverse that interval?

Have we any right to inferences? Have we any ground whatsoever for visions such as these? If we have a right to them in any degree, we have a right to their infinite extension.

The human brain has obviously a leaning to the 'infinite', and fondles the phantom of the idea. It seems to long with a passionate fervour for this impossible conception, with the hope of intellectually believing it when conceived. What is general among the whole race of man, of course no individual of that race can be warranted in considering abnormal; nevertheless, there may be a class of superior intelligences to whom the human bias alluded to may wear all the character of monomania.

My question, however, remains unanswered: 'Have we any right to infer – let us say, rather, to imagine – an interminable succession of the "clusters of clusters", or of "universes" more or less similar?'

I reply that the 'right', in a case such as this, depends absolutely upon the hardihood of that imagination which ventures to claim the right. Let me declare, only, that as an individual I myself feel impelled to the fancy – without daring to call it more – that there does exist a limitless succession of universes, more or less similar to that of which we have cognisance, to that of which alone we shall ever have cognisance, at the very least until the return of our own particular universe into unity. If such clusters of clusters exist, however – and they do – it is abundantly clear that having had no part in our origin they have no portion in our laws. They neither attract us, nor we them. Their material, their spirit is not ours – is not that which obtains in any part of our universe.

They could not impress our senses or our souls. Among them and us – considering all, for the moment, collectively – there are no influences in common. Each exists, apart and independently, in the bosom of its proper and particular God.

In the conduct of this discourse I am aiming less at physical than at metaphysical order. The clearness with which even material phenomena are presented to the understanding depends very little, I have long since learned to perceive, upon a merely natural, and almost altogether upon a moral, arrangement. If then I seem to step somewhat too discursively from point to point of my topic, let me suggest that I do so in the hope of thus the better keeping unbroken that chain of graduated impression by which alone the intellect of man can expect to encompass the grandeurs of which I speak, and, in their majestic totality, to comprehend them.

So far, our attention has been directed almost exclusively to a general and relative grouping of the stellar bodies in space. Of specification there has been little; and whatever ideas of quantity have been conveyed – that is to say, of number, magnitude, and distance – have been conveyed incidentally and by way of preparation for more definitive conceptions. These latter let us now attempt to entertain.

Our solar system, as has been already mentioned, consists in chief of one sun and seventeen planets certainly, but in all probability a few others, revolving around it as a centre, and attended by seventeen moons of which we know, with possibly several more of which as yet we know nothing. These various bodies are not true spheres, but oblate spheroids – spheres flattened at the poles of the imaginary axes about which they rotate; the flattening being a consequence of the rotation. Neither is the Sun absolutely the centre of the system; for this Sun itself, with all the planets, revolves about a perpetually shifting point of space, which is the system's general centre of gravity. Neither are we to consider the paths through which these different spheroids move – the moons about the planets, the planets about the Sun, or the Sun about the common centre – as circles in an accurate sense. They are in fact ellipses – one of the foci being the point about which the revolution is made. An ellipse is a curve returning into itself, one of whose diameters is longer than the other. In the longer diameter are two points, equidistant from the middle of the line, and so situated otherwise that, if from each of them a straight line be drawn to any one point of the curve, the two lines, taken together, will be equal to the longer diameter itself.

Now let us conceive such an ellipse. At one of the points mentioned, which are the foci, let us fasten an orange. By an elastic thread let us connect this orange with a pea, and let us place this latter on the circumference of the ellipse. Let us now move the pea continuously around the orange, keeping always on the circumference of the ellipse. The elastic thread, which of course varies in length as we move the pea, will form what in geometry is called a radius vector. Now, if the orange be understood as the Sun, and the pea as a planet revolving about it, then the revolution should be made at such a rate – with a velocity so varying – that the radius vector may pass over equal areas of space in equal times. The progress of the pea should be – in other words, the progress of the planet *is* of course – slow in proportion to its distance from the Sun, swift in proportion to its proximity. Those planets, moreover, move the more slowly which are the further from the Sun; the squares of their periods of revolution having the same proportion to each other as have to each other the cubes of their mean distances from the Sun.

The wonderfully complex laws of revolution here described, however, are not to be understood as obtaining in our system alone. They everywhere prevail where attraction prevails. They control the universe of stars. Every shining speck in the firmament is, no doubt, a luminous Sun, resembling our own, at least in its general features, and having in attendance upon it a greater or less number of planets, greater or less, whose still lingering luminosity is not sufficient to render them visible to us at so vast a distance, but which nevertheless revolve, moon-attended, about their starry centres, in obedience to the principles just detailed –

in obedience to the three omniprevalent laws of revolution, the three immortal laws *guessed* by the imaginative Kepler, and but subsequently demonstrated and accounted for by the patient and mathematical Newton. Among a tribe of philosophers who pride themselves excessively upon matter-of-fact, it is far too fashionable to sneer at all speculation under the comprehensive sobriquet, 'guess work'. The point to be considered is *who* guesses. In guessing with Plato, we spend our time to better purpose, now and then, than in harkening to a demonstration by Alcmaeon.

In many works on astronomy I find it distinctly stated that the laws of Kepler are the basis of the great principle, gravitation. This idea must have arisen from the fact that the suggestion of these laws by Kepler, and his proving them a posteriori to have an actual existence, led Newton to account for them by the hypothesis of gravitation, and finally to demonstrate them a priori, as necessary consequences of the hypothetical principle. Thus, so far from the laws of Kepler being the basis of gravity, gravity is the basis of these laws, as it is indeed of all the laws of the material universe which are not referable to repulsion alone.

The mean distance of the Earth from the Moon – that is to say, from the heavenly body in our closest vicinity – is two hundred and thirty-seven thousand miles. Mercury, the planet nearest the Sun, is distant from him thirty-seven million miles. Venus, the next, revolves at a distance of sixty-eight million; the Earth, which comes next, at a distance of ninety-five million; Mars, then, at a distance of one hundred and forty-four million. Now come the nine asteroids (Ceres, Juno, Vesta, Pallas, Astraea, Flora, Iris, Hebe, and –)[19] at an average distance of about two hundred and fifty million. Then we have Jupiter, distant four hundred and ninety million; then Saturn, nine hundred million; then Uranus, nineteen hundred million; finally Neptune, lately discovered, and revolving at a distance, say, of twenty-eight hundred million. Leaving Neptune out of the account – of which as yet we know little accurately and which is, possibly, one of a system of asteroids – it will be seen that, within certain limits, there exists an order of interval among the planets. Speaking loosely, we may say that each outer planet is twice as far from the Sun as is the next inner one. May not the order here mentioned – may not the law of Bode – be deduced from consideration of the analogy suggested by me as having place between the solar discharge of rings and the mode of the atomic radiation?

The numbers hurriedly mentioned in this summary of distance it is folly to attempt comprehending, unless in the light of abstract arithmetical facts. They are not practically tangible ones. They convey no precise ideas. I have stated that Neptune, the planet furthest from the Sun, revolves about him at a distance of twenty-eight hundred million miles. So far, good. I have stated a mathematical fact; and, without comprehending it in the least, we may put it to use – mathematically. But in mentioning, even, that the Moon revolves about the Earth at the comparatively trifling distance of two hundred and thirty-seven thousand miles, I entertained no expectation of giving any one to understand – to know, to feel – how far from the Earth the Moon actually is. Two hundred and thirty-seven thousand miles! There are, perhaps, few of my readers who have not crossed the Atlantic Ocean; yet how many of them have a distinct idea of even the three thousand miles intervening between shore and shore? I doubt, indeed, whether the man lives who can force into his brain the most remote conception of the interval between one milestone and its next neighbour upon the turnpike. We are in some measure aided, however, in our consideration of distance, by combining this consideration with the kindred one of velocity. Sound passes through eleven hundred feet of space in a second of time. Now were it possible for an inhabitant of the Earth to see the flash of a cannon discharged in the Moon, and to hear the report, he would have to wait, after perceiving the former, more than thirteen entire days and nights before getting any intimation of the latter.

However feeble be the impression, even thus conveyed, of the Moon's real distance from the Earth, it will nevertheless effect a good object in enabling us more clearly to see the futility of attempting to grasp such intervals as that of the twenty-eight hundred million miles between our Sun and Neptune; or even that of the ninety-five million between the Sun and the Earth we inhabit. A cannon-ball, flying at the greatest velocity with which a ball has ever been known to fly, could not traverse the latter interval in less than twenty years; while for the former it would require five hundred and ninety.

Our Moon's real diameter is 2,160 miles; yet she is comparatively so trifling an object that it would take nearly fifty such orbs to compose one as great as the Earth.

The diameter of our own globe is 7,912 miles; but from the enunciation of these numbers what positive idea do we derive?

If we ascend an ordinary mountain and look around us from its summit, we behold a landscape stretching, say, forty miles in every direction, forming a circle two hundred and fifty miles in circumference, and including an area of five thousand square miles. The extent of such a prospect, on account of the successiveness with which its portions necessarily present themselves to view, can be only very feebly and very partially appreciated; yet the entire panorama would comprehend no more than one forty-thousandth part of the mere surface of our globe. Were this panorama, then, to be succeeded after the lapse of an hour by another of equal extent; this again by a third after the lapse of another hour; this again by a fourth, after the lapse of another hour – and so on, until the scenery of the whole Earth were exhausted; and were we to be engaged in examining these various panoramas for twelve hours of every day; we should, nevertheless, be nine years and forty-eight days in completing the general survey.

But if the mere surface of the Earth eludes the grasp of the imagination, what are we to think of its cubical contents? It embraces a mass of matter equal in weight to at least two sextillions, two hundred quintillions of tons. Let us suppose it in a state of quiescence; and now let us endeavour to conceive a mechanical force sufficient to set it in motion! Not the strength of all the myriads of beings whom we may conclude to inhabit the planetary worlds of our system, not the combined physical strength of all these beings – even admitting all to be more powerful than man – would avail to stir the ponderous mass a single inch from its position.

What are we to understand, then, of the force which under similar circumstances would be required to move the largest of our planets, Jupiter? This is eighty-six thousand miles in diameter, and would include within its surface more than a thousand orbs of the magnitude of our own. Yet this stupendous body is actually flying around the Sun at the rate of twenty-nine thousand miles an hour – that is to say, with a velocity forty times greater than that of a cannon-ball! The thought of such a phenomenon cannot well be said to startle the mind – it palsies and appals it. Not infrequently we task our imagination in picturing the capacities of an angel. Let us fancy such a being at a distance of some hundred miles from Jupiter, a close eyewitness of this planet as it speeds on its annual revolution. Now can we, I demand, fashion for ourselves any conception so distinct of this ideal being's spiritual exaltation, as that involved in the supposition that, even by this immeasurable mass of matter whirled immediately before his eyes, with a velocity so unutterable, he, an angel – angelic though he be – is not at once struck into nothingness and overwhelmed?

At this point, however, it seems proper to suggest that, in fact, we have been speaking of comparative trifles. Our Sun – the central and controlling orb of the system to which Jupiter belongs – is not only greater than Jupiter, but greater by far than all the planets of the system taken together. This fact is an essential condition, indeed, of the stability of the system itself. The diameter of Jupiter has been mentioned: it is eighty-six thousand miles; that of the Sun is eight hundred and eighty-two thousand miles. An inhabitant of the latter, travelling ninety miles a day, would be more than eighty years in going round a great circle of its circumference. It occupies a cubical space of 681 quadrillions, 472 trillions of miles. The Moon, as has been stated, revolves about the Earth at a distance of two hundred and thirty-seven thousand miles – in an orbit, consequently, of nearly a million and a half. Now, were the Sun placed upon the Earth, centre over centre, the body of the former would extend, in every direction, not only to the line of the Moon's orbit, but beyond it a distance of two hundred thousand miles.

And here, once again, let me suggest that in fact we have still been speaking of comparative trifles. The distance of the planet Neptune from the Sun has been stated; it is twenty hundred million miles; its orbit, therefore, is about seventeen billions. Let this be borne in mind while we glance at one of the brightest stars. Between this and the star of our system (the Sun) there is a gulf of space, to convey any idea of which we should need the tongue of an archangel. From our system, then, and from our Sun, or star, the star at which we suppose ourselves glancing is a thing altogether apart. Still, for the moment, let us imagine it placed upon our Sun, centre over centre, as we just now imagined this Sun itself placed upon the Earth. Let us now conceive the particular star we have in mind, extending, in every direction, beyond the orbit of Mercury, of Venus, of the Earth – still on, beyond the orbit of Mars, of the asteroids, of Jupiter, of Saturn, of Uranus – until, finally, we fancy it filling the circle, seventeen billions of miles in circumference, which is described by the revolution of Leverrier's planet. When we have conceived all this, we shall have entertained no extravagant conception. There is the very best reason for believing that many of the stars are even far larger than the one we have imagined. I mean to say that we have the very best empirical basis for such belief. And in looking back at the original, atomic arrangements for diversity, which have been assumed as a part of the divine plan in the constitution of the universe, we shall be enabled easily to understand, and to credit, the existence of even far vaster disproportions in stellar size than any to which I have hitherto alluded. The largest orbs, of course, we must expect to find rolling through the widest vacancies of space.

I remarked just now that to convey an idea of the interval between our Sun and any one of the other stars we should require the eloquence of an archangel. In so saying, I should not be accused of exaggeration; for in simple truth these are topics on which it is scarcely possible to exaggerate. But let us bring the matter more distinctly before the eye of the mind.

In the first place, we may get a general, relative conception of the interval referred to, by comparing it with the interplanetary spaces. If, for example, we suppose the Earth, which is in reality ninety-five million miles from the Sun, to be only one foot from that luminary, then Neptune would be forty feet distant, and the star, Alpha Lyrae, at the very least, one hundred and fifty-nine.

Now, I presume that in the termination of my last sentence few of my readers have noticed anything specially objectionable – particularly wrong. I said that the distance of the Earth from the Sun being taken at one foot, the distance of Neptune would be forty feet, and that of Alpha Lyrae one hundred and fifty-nine. The proportion between one foot and one hundred and fifty-nine has appeared, perhaps, to convey a sufficiently definite impression of the proportion between the two intervals – that of the Earth from the Sun, and that of Alpha Lyrae from the same luminary. But my account of the matter should, in reality, have run thus: the distance of the Earth from the Sun being taken at one foot, the distance of Neptune would be forty feet, and that of Alpha Lyrae one hundred and fifty-nine – *miles*. That is to say, I had assigned to Alpha Lyrae, in my first statement of the case, only the 5280th part of that distance which is the least distance possible at which it can actually lie.

To proceed: however distant a mere planet is, yet when we look at it through a telescope we see it under a certain form – of a certain appreciable size. Now I have already hinted at the probable bulk of many of the stars; nevertheless, when we view any one of them, even through the most powerful telescope, it is found to present us with no form, and consequently with no magnitude whatsoever. We see it as a point and nothing more.

Again, let us suppose ourselves walking, at night, on a highway. In a field on one side of the road is a line of tall objects, say trees, the figures of which are distinctly defined against the background of the sky. This line of objects extends at right angles to the road, and from the road to the horizon. Now, as we proceed along the road, we see these objects changing their positions, respectively, in relation to a certain fixed point in that portion of the firmament which forms the background of the view. Let us suppose this fixed point – sufficiently fixed for our purpose – to be the rising moon. We become aware, at once, that while the tree nearest us so far alters its position, in respect to the moon, as to seem flying behind us, the tree in the extreme distance has scarcely changed at all its relative position with the satellite. We then go on to perceive that the further the objects are from us, the less they alter their positions, and the converse. Then we begin, unwittingly, to estimate the distances of individual trees by the degrees in which they evince the relative alteration. Finally, we come to understand how it might be possible to ascertain the actual distance of any given tree in the line by using the amount of relative alteration as a basis in a simple geometrical problem. Now, this relative alteration is what we call 'parallax'; and by parallax we calculate the distances of the heavenly bodies. Applying the principle to the trees in question, we should of course be very much at a loss to comprehend the distance of that tree, which, however far we proceeded along the road, should evince no parallax at all. This, in the case described, is a thing impossible; but impossible only because all distances on our Earth are trivial indeed. In comparison with the vast cosmic quantities, we may speak of them as absolutely nothing.

Now, let us suppose the star Alpha Lyrae directly overhead, and let us imagine that instead of standing on the Earth we stand at one end of a straight road stretching through space to a distance equalling the diameter of the Earth's orbit – that is to say, to a distance of one hundred and ninety million miles. Having observed, by means of the most delicate micrometrical instruments, the exact position of the star, let us now pass along this inconceivable road until we reach its other extremity. Now, once again, let us look at the star. It is precisely where we left it. Our instruments, however delicate, assure us that its relative position is absolutely – is identically – the same as at the commencement of our unutterable journey. No parallax – none whatever – has been found.

The fact is that in regard to the distance of the fixed stars – of any one of the myriads of suns glistening on the further side of that awful chasm which separates our system from its brothers in the cluster to which it belongs – astronomical science, until very lately, could speak only with a negative certainty. Assuming the brightest as the nearest, we could say, even of them, only that there is a certain incomprehensible distance on the hither side of which they cannot be. How far they are beyond it we had in no case been able to ascertain. We perceived, for example, that Alpha Lyrae cannot be nearer to us than nineteen trillions, two hundred billions of miles; but, for all we knew, and indeed for all we now know, it may be distant from us the square, or the cube, or any other power of the number mentioned. By dint, however, of wonderfully minute and cautious observations continued, with novel instruments, for many laborious years, Bessel, not long ago deceased, has lately succeeded in determining the distance of six or seven stars; among others, that of the star numbered 61 in the constellation of the Swan. The distance in this latter instance ascertained, is six hundred and seventy thousand times that of the Sun; which last, it will be remembered, is ninety-five million miles. The star 61 Cygni, then, is nearly sixty-four trillions of miles from us – or more than three times the distance assigned, as the least possible, for Alpha Lyrae.

In attempting to appreciate this interval by the aid of any considerations of velocity, as we did in endeavouring to estimate the distance of the Moon, we must leave out of sight, altogether, such nothings as the speed of a cannon-ball, or of sound. Light, however, according to the latest calculations of Struve, proceeds at the rate of one hundred and sixty-seven thousand miles in a second. Thought itself cannot pass through this interval more speedily – if, indeed, thought can traverse it at all. Yet, in coming from 61 Cygni to us, even at this inconceivable rate, light occupies more than ten years. And, consequently, were the star this moment blotted out from the universe, still, for ten years, would it continue to sparkle on, undimmed in its paradoxical glory.

Keeping now in mind whatever feeble conception we may have attained of the interval between our Sun and 61 Cygni, let us remember that this interval, however unutterably vast, we are permitted to consider as but the average interval among the countless host of stars composing that cluster, or 'nebula', to which our system, as well as that of 61 Cygni, belongs. I have, in fact, stated the case with great moderation. We have excellent reason for believing 61 Cygni to be one of the nearest stars, and thus for concluding, at least for the present, that its distance from us is less than the average distance between star and star in the magnificent cluster of the Milky Way.

And here, once again and finally, it seems proper to suggest that even as yet we have been speaking of trifles. Ceasing to wonder at the space between star and star in our own or in any particular cluster, let us rather turn our thoughts to the intervals between cluster and cluster in the all-comprehensive cluster of the universe.

I have already said that light proceeds at the rate of one hundred and sixty-seven thousand miles in a second – that is, about ten million miles in a minute, or about six hundred million miles in an hour. Yet so far removed from us are some of the 'nebulae' that even light, speeding with this velocity, could not and does not reach us from those mysterious regions in less than three million years. This calculation, moreover, is made by the Elder Herschel, and in reference merely to those comparatively proximate clusters within the scope of his own telescope. There are 'nebulae', however, which, through the magical tube of Lord Rosse, are this instant whispering in our ears the secrets of a million ages gone by. In a word, the events which we behold now – at this moment – in those worlds are the identical events which interested their inhabitants ten hundred thousand centuries ago. In intervals, in distances, such as this suggestion forces upon the soul rather than upon the mind, we find at length a fitting climax to all hitherto frivolous considerations of quantity.

Our fancies thus occupied with the cosmic distances, let us

take the opportunity of referring to the difficulty which we have so often experienced, while pursuing the beaten path of astronomical reflection in accounting for the immeasurable voids alluded to; in comprehending why chasms so totally unoccupied and therefore apparently so needless, have been made to intervene between star and star, between cluster and cluster; in understanding, to be brief, a sufficient reason for the titanic scale, in respect of mere space, on which the universe of stars is seen to be constructed. A rational cause for the phenomenon, I maintain that astronomy has palpably failed to assign; but the considerations through which, in this essay, we have proceeded step by step, enable us clearly and immediately to perceive that space and duration are one. That the universe might endure throughout an era at all commensurate with the grandeur of its component material portions and with the high majesty of its spiritual purposes, it was necessary that the original atomic diffusion be made to so inconceivable an extent as to be only not infinite. It was required, in a word, that the stars should be gathered into visibility from invisible nebulosity – proceed from visibility to consolidation – and so grow grey in giving birth and death to unspeakably numerous and complex variations of vital development. It was required that the stars should do all this – should have time thoroughly to accomplish all these divine purposes – during the period in which all things were effecting their return into unity with a velocity accumulating in the inverse proportion of the squares of the distances at which lay the inevitable end.

Throughout all this we have no difficulty in understanding the absolute accuracy of the divine adaptation. The density of the stars, respectively, proceeds of course as their condensation diminishes; condensation and heterogeneity keep pace with each other. Through the latter, which is the index of the former, we estimate the vital and spiritual development. Thus, in the density of the globes, we have the measure in which their purposes are fulfilled. As density proceeds – as the divine intentions are accomplished, as less and still less remains to be accomplished – so, in the same ratio, should we expect to find an acceleration of the end. And thus the philosophical mind will easily comprehend that the divine designs in constituting the stars advance mathematically to their fulfilment – and more, it will readily give the advance a mathematical expression, it will decide that this advance is inversely proportional with the squares of the distances of all created things from the starting-point and goal of their creation.

Not only is this divine adaptation, however, mathematically accurate, but there is that about it which stamps it as divine, in distinction from that which is merely the work of human constructiveness. I allude to the complete mutuality of adaptation. For example, in human constructions a particular cause has a particular effect; a particular intention brings to pass a particular object, but this is all; we see no reciprocity. The effect does not react upon the cause; the intention does not change relations with the object. In divine constructions the object is either design or object as we choose to regard it – and we may take at any time a cause for an effect, or the converse – so that we can never absolutely decide which is which.

To give an instance: in polar climates the human frame, to maintain its animal heat, requires for combustion in the capillary system an abundant supply of highly azotised food, such as train oil. But again, in polar climates nearly the sole food afforded man is the oil of abundant seals and whales. Now, is oil at hand because imperatively demanded, or the only thing demanded because the only thing to be obtained? It is impossible to decide. There is an absolute reciprocity of adaptation.

The pleasure which we derive from any display of human ingenuity is in the ratio of the approach to this species of reciprocity. In the construction of plot, for example, in fictitious literature, we should aim at so arranging the incidents that we shall not be able to determine, of any one of them, whether it depends from any one other or upholds it. In this sense, of course, perfection of plot is really, or practically, unattainable – but only because it is a finite intelligence that constructs. The plots of God are perfect. The universe is a plot of God.

And now we have reached a point at which the intellect is forced, again, to struggle against its propensity for analogical inference – against its monomaniac grasping at the infinite. Moons have been seen revolving about planets; planets about stars; and the poetical instinct of humanity – its instinct of the symmetrical, even if the symmetry be but a symmetry of surface; this instinct which the soul, not only of man but of all created beings, took up in the beginning from the geometrical basis of the universal radiation – impels us to the fancy of an endless extension of this system of cycles. Closing our eyes equally to deduction and induction, we insist upon imagining a revolution of all the orbs of the galaxy about some gigantic globe which we take to be the central pivot of the whole. Each cluster in the great cluster of clusters is imagined, of course, to be similarly supplied and constructed, while, that the 'analogy' may be wanting at no point, we go on to conceive these clusters themselves, again, as revolving about some still more august sphere – this latter, still again, with its encircling clusters, as but one of a yet more magnificent series of agglomerations, gyrating about yet another orb central to them, some orb still more unspeakably sublime, some orb, let us rather say, of infinite sublimity, endlessly multiplied by the infinitely sublime. Such are the conditions, continued in perpetuity, which the voice of what some people term 'analogy' calls upon the fancy to depict and the reason to contemplate, if possible, without becoming dissatisfied with the picture. Such, in general, are the interminable gyrations beyond gyration which we have been instructed by philosophy to comprehend and to account for – at least in the best manner we can. Now and then, however, a philosopher proper – one whose frenzy takes a very determinate turn, whose genius, to speak more reverentially, has a strongly pronounced washerwoman-ish bias, doing everything up by the dozen – enables us to see precisely that point out of sight at which the revolutionary processes in question do, and of right ought to, come to an end.

It is hardly worthwhile, perhaps, even to sneer at the reveries of Fourier; but much has been said, latterly, of the hypothesis of

Mädler – that there exists in the centre of the galaxy a stupendous globe about which all the systems of the cluster revolve. The period of our own, indeed, has been stated – one hundred and seventeen million years.

That our Sun has a motion in space, independently of its rotation, and revolution about the system's centre of gravity, has long been suspected. This motion, granting it to exist, would be manifested perspectively. The stars in that firmamental region which we were leaving behind us, would, in a very long series of years, become crowded; those in the opposite quarter, scattered. Now, by means of astronomical history, we ascertain, cloudily, that some such phenomena have occurred. On this ground it has been declared that our system is moving to a point in the heavens diametrically opposite the star Zeta Herculis. But this inference is perhaps the maximum to which we have any logical right. Mädler, however, has gone so far as to designate a particular star, Alcyone in the Pleiades, as being at or about the very spot around which a general revolution is performed.

Now, since by 'analogy' we are led, in the first instance, to these dreams, it is no more than proper that we should abide by analogy, at least in some measure, during their development; and that analogy which suggests the revolution suggests at the same time a central orb about which it should be performed. So far the astronomer was consistent. This central orb, however, should dynamically be greater than all the orbs taken together which surround it. Of these there are about one hundred million. 'Why, then,' it was of course demanded, 'do we not *see* this vast central sun? At least equal in mass to one hundred million suns such as ours, why do we not see it – we, especially, who occupy the mid region of the cluster, the very locality near which, at all events, must be situated this incomparable star?' The reply was ready. 'It must be non-luminous, as are our planets.' Here, then, to suit a purpose, analogy is suddenly let fall. 'Not so,' it may be said, 'we know that non-luminous suns actually exist.' It is true that we have reason at least for supposing so; but we have certainly no reason whatever for supposing that the non-luminous suns in question are encircled by luminous suns, while these again are surrounded by non-luminous planets. And it is precisely all this with which Mädler is called upon to find anything analogous in the heavens – for it is precisely all this which he imagines in the case of the galaxy. Admitting the thing to be so, we cannot help here picturing to ourselves how sad a puzzle the 'why is it so?' must prove to all a-priori philosophers.

But granting, in the very teeth of analogy and of everything else, the non-luminosity of the vast central orb, we may still enquire how this orb, so enormous, could fail of being rendered visible by the flood of light thrown upon it from the one hundred million glorious suns glaring in all directions about it. On the urging of this question, the idea of an actually solid central sun appears, in some measure, to have been abandoned, and spec- ulation proceeded to assert that the systems of the cluster perform their revolutions merely about an immaterial centre of gravity common to all. Here again, then, to suit a purpose, analogy is let fall. The planets of our system revolve, it is true, about a common centre of gravity; but they do this in connection with, and in consequence of, a material sun whose mass more than counterbalances the rest of the system.

The mathematical circle is a curve composed of an infinity of straight lines. But this idea of the circle – an idea, which in view of all ordinary geometry, is merely the mathematical, as counter- distinguished from the practical, idea – is in sober fact the practical conception which alone we have any right to entertain in regard to the majestic circle with which we have to deal, at least in fancy, when we suppose our system revolving about a point in the centre of the galaxy. Let the most vigorous of human imaginations attempt but to take a single step towards the comprehension of a sweep so ineffable! It would scarcely be paradoxical to say that a flash of lightning itself, travelling forever upon the circumference of this unutterable circle, would still, forever, be travelling in a straight line. That the path of our Sun in such an orbit would, to any human perception, deviate in the slightest degree from a straight line, even in a million years, is a proposition not to be entertained. Yet we are required to believe that a curvature has become apparent during the brief period of our astronomical history – during a mere point – during the utter nothingness of two or three thousand years.

It may be said that Mädler has really ascertained a curvature in the direction of our system's now well-established progress through space. Admitting, if necessary, this fact to be in reality such, I maintain that nothing is thereby shown except the reality of this fact – the fact of a curvature. For its thorough determination, ages will be required; and, when determined, it will be found indicative of some binary or other multiple relation between our Sun and some one or more of the proximate stars. I hazard nothing, however, in predicting that after the lapse of many centuries all efforts at determining the path of our sun through Space will be abandoned as fruitless. This is easily conceivable when we look at the infinity of perturbation it must experience from its perpetually shifting relations with other orbs, in the common approach of all to the nucleus of the galaxy.

But in examining other 'nebulae' than that of the Milky Way – in surveying, generally, the clusters which overspread the heavens – do we or do we not find confirmation of Mädler's hypothesis? We do not. The forms of the clusters are exceedingly diverse when casually viewed; but on close inspection, through powerful telescopes, we recognise the sphere, very distinctly, as at least the proximate form of all; their constitution, in general, being at variance with the idea of revolution about a common centre.

'It is difficult,' says Sir John Herschel, 'to form any conception of the dynamical state of such systems. On one hand, without a rotary motion and a centrifugal force, it is hardly possible not to regard them as in a state of progressive collapse. On the other, granting such a motion and such a force, we find it no less difficult to reconcile their forms with the rotation of the whole system [meaning cluster] around any single axis, without which internal collision would appear to be inevitable.'

Some remarks lately made about the 'nebulae' by Dr Nichol, in taking quite a different view of the cosmic conditions from any taken in this discourse, have a very peculiar applicability to the point now at issue. He says:

'When our greatest telescopes are brought to bear upon them, we find that those which were thought to be irregular are not so; they approach nearer to a globe. Here is one that looked oval; but Lord Rosse's telescope brought it into a circle... Now there occurs a very remarkable circumstance in reference to these comparatively sweeping circular masses of nebulae. We find they are not entirely circular, but the reverse. And that all around them, on every side, there are volumes of stars, stretching out apparently as if they were rushing towards a great central mass in consequence of the action of some great power.'[20]

Were I to describe, in my own words, what must necessarily be the existing condition of each nebula, on the hypothesis that all matter is, as I suggest, now returning to its original unity, I should simply be going over, nearly verbatim, the language here employed by Dr Nichol, without the faintest suspicion of that stupendous truth which is the key to these nebular phenomena.

And here let me fortify my position still further by the voice of one greater than Mädler; of one, moreover, to whom all the data of Mädler have long been familiar things, carefully and thoroughly considered. Referring to the elaborate calculations of Argelander – the very researches which form Mädler's basis – Humboldt, whose generalising powers have never perhaps been equalled, has the following observation:

'When we regard the real, proper, or non-perspective motions of the stars, we find many groups of them moving in opposite directions; and the data as yet in hand render it not necessary, at least, to conceive that the systems composing the Milky Way, or the clusters, generally, composing the universe, are revolving about any particular centre unknown, whether luminous or non-luminous. It is but man's longing for a fundamental first cause that impels both his intellect and fancy to the adoption of such a hypothesis.'

The phenomenon here alluded to – that of 'many groups moving in opposite directions' – is quite inexplicable by Mädler's idea, but arises as a necessary consequence from that which forms the basis of this discourse. While the *merely general direction* of each atom – of each moon, planet, star, or cluster – would on my hypothesis be of course absolutely rectilinear, while the *general* path of all bodies would be a right line leading to the centre of all, it is clear nevertheless that this general rectilinearity would be compounded of what, with scarcely any exaggeration, we may term an infinity of particular curves – an infinity of local deviations from rectilinearity – the result of continuous differences of relative position among the multitudinous masses, as each proceeds on its own proper journey to the end.

I quoted, just now, from Sir John Herschel, the following words, used in reference to the clusters: 'On one hand, without a rotary motion and a centrifugal force, it is hardly possible not to regard them as in a state of progressive collapse.' The fact is that in surveying the 'nebulae' with a telescope of high power, we shall find it quite impossible, having once conceived this idea of 'collapse', not to gather at all points corroboration of the idea. A nucleus is always apparent in the direction of which the stars seem to be precipitating themselves. Nor can these nuclei be mistaken for merely perspective phenomena; the clusters are really denser near the centre, sparser in the regions more remote from it. In a word, we see everything as we should see it were a collapse taking place; but, in general, it may be said of these clusters that we can fairly entertain, while looking at them, the idea of orbital movement about a centre, only by admitting the possible existence, in the distant domains of space, of dynamical laws with which we are unacquainted.

On the part of Herschel, however, there is evidently a reluctance to regard the nebulae as in 'a state of progressive collapse'. But if facts – if even appearances justify the supposition of their being in this state – *why*, it may well be demanded, is he disinclined to admit it? Simply on account of a prejudice. Merely because the supposition is at war with a preconceived and utterly baseless notion – that of the endlessness, that of the eternal stability of the universe.

If the propositions of this discourse are tenable, the 'state of progressive collapse' is precisely that state in which alone we are warranted in considering all things. And, with due humility, let me here confess that, for my part, I am at a loss to conceive how any other understanding of the existing condition of affairs could ever have made its way into the human brain. 'The tendency to collapse' and 'the attraction of gravitation' are convertible phrases. In using either, we speak of the reaction of the first act. Never was necessity less obvious than that of supposing matter imbued with an ineradicable quality forming part of its material nature – a quality, or instinct, forever inseparable from it, and by dint of which inalienable principle every atom is perpetually impelled to seek its fellow-atom. Never was necessity less obvious than that of entertaining this unphilosophical idea. Going boldly behind the vulgar thought, we have to conceive, metaphysically, that the gravitating principle appertains to matter temporarily, only while diffused, only while existing as many instead of as one, appertains to it by virtue of its state of radiation alone – appertains, in a word, altogether to its *condition*, and not in the slightest degree to *itself*. In this view, when the radiation shall have returned into its source – when the reaction shall be completed – the gravitating principle will no longer exist. And, in fact, astronomers, without at any time reaching the idea here suggested, seem to have been approximating it in the assertion that 'if there were but one body in the universe, it would be impossible to understand how the principle, gravity, could obtain' – that is to say, from a consideration of matter as they find it, they reach a conclusion at which I deductively arrive. That so pregnant a suggestion as the one quoted should have been permitted to remain so long unfruitful, is nevertheless a mystery which I find it difficult to fathom.

It is perhaps in no little degree, however, our propensity for the continuous, for the analogical – in the present case more particularly for the symmetrical – which has been leading us astray. And, in fact, the sense of the symmetrical is an instinct which may be depended on with an almost blindfold reliance. It is the poetical essence of the universe – *of the universe* which, in the supremeness of its symmetry, is but the most sublime of poems. Now, symmetry and consistency are convertible terms; thus poetry and truth are one. A thing is consistent in the ratio of its truth, true in the ratio of its consistency. A perfect consistency, I repeat, can be nothing but an absolute truth. We may take it for granted, then, that man cannot long or widely err if he suffer himself to be guided by his poetical, which I have maintained to be his truthful, in being his symmetrical, instinct. He must have a care, however, lest in pursuing too heedlessly the superficial symmetry of forms and motions he leave out of sight the really essential symmetry of the principles which determine and control them.

That the stellar bodies would finally be merged in one – that, at last, all would be drawn into the substance of one stupendous central orb already existing – is an idea which for some time past seems, vaguely and indeterminately, to have held possession of the fancy of mankind. It is an idea, in fact, which belongs to the class of the excessively obvious. It springs instantly from a superficial observation of the cyclic and seemingly gyrating or vortical movements of those individual portions of the universe which come most immediately and most closely under our observation. There is not perhaps a human being of ordinary education and of average reflective capacity to whom, at some period, the fancy in question has not occurred, as if spontaneously, or intuitively, and wearing all the character of a very profound and very original conception. This conception, however, so commonly entertained, has never, within my knowledge, arisen out of any abstract considerations. Being on the contrary always suggested, as I say, by the vortical movements about centres, a reason for it, also – a cause for the in-gathering of all the orbs into one, imagined to be already existing – was naturally sought in the same direction among these cyclic movements themselves.

Thus it happened that, on announcement of the gradual and perfectly regular decrease observed in the orbit of Encke's comet, at every successive revolution about our Sun, astronomers were nearly unanimous in the opinion that the cause in question was found, that a principle was discovered sufficient to account, physically, for that final, universal agglomeration which, I repeat, the analogical, symmetrical, or poetical instinct of man had predetermined to understand as something more than a simple hypothesis.

This cause, this sufficient reason for the final in-gathering, was declared to exist in an exceedingly rare but still material medium pervading space; which medium, by retarding in some degree the progress of the comet, perpetually weakened its tangential force, thus giving a predominance to the centripetal, which of course drew the comet nearer and nearer at each revolution, and would eventually precipitate it upon the Sun.

All this was strictly logical – admitting the medium or ether. But this ether was assumed, most illogically, on the grounds that no other mode than the one spoken of could be discovered, of accounting for the observed decrease in the orbit of the comet, as if from the fact that we could discover no other mode of accounting for it, it followed in any respect that no other mode of accounting for it existed. It is clear that innumerable causes might operate, in combination, to diminish the orbit, without even a possibility of our ever becoming acquainted with one of them. In the meantime, it has never been fairly shown, perhaps, why the retardation occasioned by the skirts of the Sun's atmosphere, through which the comet passes at perihelion, is not enough to account for the phenomenon. That Encke's comet will be absorbed into the Sun is probable. That all the comets of the system will be absorbed is more than merely possible. But, in such case, the principle of absorption must be referred to eccentricity of orbit – to the close approximation to the Sun of the comets at their perihelia; and a principle not affecting, in any degree, the ponderous spheres which are to be regarded as the true material constituents of the universe. Touching comets in general, let me here suggest, in passing, that we cannot be far wrong in looking upon them as the lightning flashes of the cosmic heaven.

The idea of a retarding ether and, through it, of a final agglomeration of all things, seemed at one time, however, to be confirmed by the observation of a positive decrease in the orbit of the solid Moon. By reference to eclipses recorded twenty-five hundred years ago, it was found that the velocity of the satellite's revolution then was considerably less than it is now; that on the hypothesis that its motion in its orbit is uniformly in accordance with Kepler's law, and was accurately determined then – twenty-five hundred years ago – it is now in advance of the position it should occupy, by nearly nine thousand miles. The increase of velocity proved, of course, a diminution of orbit, and astronomers were fast yielding to a belief in an ether as the sole mode of accounting for the phenomenon, when Lagrange came to the rescue. He showed that, owing to the configurations of the spheroids, the shorter axes of their ellipses are subject to variation in length; the longer axes being permanent; and that this variation is continuous and vibratory – so that every orbit is in a state of transition, either from circle to ellipse, or from ellipse to circle. In the case of the Moon, where the shorter axis is decreasing, the orbit is passing from circle to ellipse, and con-sequently is decreasing too. But, after a long series of ages, the ultimate eccentricity will be attained; then the shorter axis will proceed to increase, until the orbit becomes a circle; when the process of shortening will again take place. And so on forever. In the case of the Earth, the orbit is passing from ellipse to circle. The facts thus demonstrated do away, of course, with all necessity for supposing an ether, and with all apprehension of the system's instability – on the ether's account.

It will be remembered that I have myself assumed what we may term an ether. I have spoken of a subtle influence which we know to be ever in attendance on matter, although becoming manifest only through matter's heterogeneity. To this influence – without daring to touch it at all in any effort at explaining its awful nature – I have referred the various phenomena of electricity, heat, light, magnetism, and more – of vitality, consciousness, and thought – in a word, of spirituality. It will be seen at once then, that the ether thus conceived is radically distinct from the ether of the astronomers, inasmuch as theirs is matter and mine not.

With the idea of material ether, seems thus to have departed altogether the thought of that universal agglomeration so long predetermined by the poetical fancy of mankind; an agglomeration in which a sound philosophy might have been warranted in putting faith, at least to a certain extent, if for no other reason than that by this poetical fancy it had been so predetermined. But so far as astronomy, so far as mere physics, have yet spoken, the cycles of the universe are perpetual. The universe has no conceivable end. Had an end been demonstrated, however, from so purely collateral a cause as an ether, man's instinct of the divine capacity to adapt would have rebelled against the demonstration. We should have been forced to regard the universe with some such sense of dissatisfaction as we experience in contemplating an unnecessarily complex work of human art. Creation would have affected us as an imperfect plot in a romance, where the denouement is awkwardly brought about by interposed incidents external and foreign to the main subject, instead of springing out of the bosom of the thesis, out of the heart of the ruling idea, instead of arising as a result of the primary proposition, as inseparable and inevitable part and parcel of the fundamental conception of the book.

What I mean by the symmetry of mere surface will now be more clearly understood. It is simply by the blandishment of this symmetry that we have been beguiled into the general idea of which Mädler's hypothesis is but a part – the idea of the vortical in-drawing of the orbs. Dismissing this nakedly physical conception, the symmetry of principle sees the end of all things metaphysically involved in the thought of a beginning; seeks and finds, in this origin of all things, the rudiment of this end; and perceives the impiety of supposing this end likely to be brought about less simply, less directly, less obviously, less artistically than through the reaction of the originating act.

Recurring, then, to a previous suggestion, let us understand the systems – let us understand each star, with its attendant planets – as but a titanic atom existing in space with precisely the same inclination for unity which characterised, in the beginning, the actual atoms after their radiation throughout the universal sphere. As these original atoms rushed towards each other in generally straight lines, so let us conceive as at least generally rectilinear the paths of the system-atoms towards their respective centres of aggregation. And in this direct drawing together of the systems into clusters, with a similar and simultaneous drawing together of the clusters themselves while undergoing con-solidation, we have at length attained the great now – the awful present – the existing condition of the universe.

Of the still more awful future a not irrational analogy may guide us in framing a hypothesis. The equilibrium between the centripetal and centrifugal forces of each system, being neces-sarily destroyed on attainment of a certain proximity to the nucleus of the cluster to which it belongs, there must occur at once a chaotic or seemingly chaotic precipitation of the moons upon the planets, of the planets upon the suns, and of the suns upon the nuclei. And the general result of this precipitation must be the gathering of the myriad now-existing stars of the firmament into an almost infinitely less number of almost infinitely superior spheres. In being immeasurably fewer, the worlds of that day will be immeasurably greater than our own. Then, indeed, amid unfathomable abysses, will be glaring unimaginable suns. But all this will be merely a climatic magni-ficence foreboding the great end. Of this end the new genesis described can be but a very partial postponement. While under-going consolidation, the clusters themselves, with a speed prodigiously accumulative, have been rushing towards their own general centre – and now, with a million-fold electric velocity, commensurate only with their material grandeur and with their spiritual passion for oneness, the majestic remnants of the tribe of stars flash, at length, into a common embrace. The inevitable catastrophe is at hand.

But this catastrophe – what is it? We have seen accomplished the in-gathering of the orbs. Henceforward, are we not to understand one material globe of globes as comprehending and constituting the universe? Such a fancy would be altogether at war with every assumption and consideration of this discourse.

I have already alluded to that absolute reciprocity of adaptation which is the idiosyncrasy of the divine art – stamping it divine. Up to this point of our reflections, we have been regarding the electrical influence as something by dint of whose repulsion alone matter is enabled to exist in that state of diffusion demanded for the fulfilment of its purposes. So far, in a word, we have been considering the influence in question as ordained for matter's sake – to subserve the objects of matter. With a perfectly legitimate reciprocity, we are now permitted to look at matter as created solely for the sake of this influence – solely to serve the objects of this spiritual ether. Through the aid, by the means, through the agency of matter, and by dint of its heterogeneity, is this ether manifested – is spirit individualised. It is merely in the development of this ether, through heterogeneity, that particular masses of matter become animate – sensitive – and in the ratio of their heterogeneity; some reaching a degree of sensitiveness involving what we call thought, and thus attaining obviously conscious intelligence.

In this view, we are enabled to perceive matter as a means, not as an end. Its purposes are thus seen to have been comprehended in its diffusion; and with the return into unity these purposes cease. The absolutely consolidated globe of globes would be objectless, therefore not for a moment could it continue to exist. Matter, created for an end, would unquestionably, on fulfilment of that end, be matter no longer. Let us endeavour to understand that it would disappear, and that God would remain all in all.

That every work of divine conception must coexist and co-expire with its particular design, seems to me especially obvious, and I make no doubt that, on perceiving the final globe of globes to be objectless, the majority of my readers will be satisfied with my '*therefore* it cannot continue to exist'. Nevertheless, as the startling thought of its instantaneous disappearance is one which the most powerful intellect cannot be expected readily to entertain on grounds so decidedly abstract, let us endeavour to look at the idea from another and more ordinary point of view. Let us see how thoroughly and beautifully it is corroborated in an a-posteriori consideration of matter as we actually find it.

I have before said that attraction and repulsion being undeniably the sole properties by which matter is manifested to mind, we are justified in assuming that matter exists only as attraction and repulsion. In other words, that attraction and repulsion *are* matter, there being no conceivable case in which we may not employ the term 'matter' and the terms 'attraction' and 'repulsion', taken together, as equivalent, and therefore convertible, expressions of logic.[21]

Now the very definition of attraction implies particularity – the existence of parts, particles, or atoms; for we define it as the tendency of 'each atom, etc., to every other atom, etc.,' according to a certain law. Of course where there are no parts, where there is absolute unity, where the tendency to oneness is satisfied, there can be no attraction. This has been fully shown, and all philosophy admits it. When, on fulfilment of its purposes, then, matter shall have returned into its original condition of one (a condition which presupposes the expulsion of the separative ether whose province and whose capacity are limited to keeping the atoms apart until that great day when, this ether being no longer needed, the overwhelming pressure of the finally collective attraction shall at length just sufficiently predominate and expel it[22]), when, I say, matter, finally expelling the ether shall have returned into absolute unity, it will then (to speak paradoxically for the moment) be matter without attraction and without repulsion: in other words, matter without matter; in other words, again, matter no more. In sinking into unity it will sink at once into that nothingness which, to all finite perception, unity must be, into that material nihility from which alone we can conceive it to have been evoked, to have been created, by the volition of God. I repeat, then, let us endeavour to comprehend that the final globe of globes will instantaneously disappear, and that God will remain all in all.

But are we here to pause? Not so. On the universal agglomeration and dissolution, we can readily conceive that a new and perhaps totally different series of conditions may ensue; another creation and radiation, returning into itself; another action and reaction of the divine will. Guiding our imaginations by that omniprevalent law of laws, the law of periodicity, are we not, indeed, more than justified in entertaining a belief – let us say, rather, in indulging a hope – that the processes we have here ventured to contemplate will be renewed forever, and forever, and forever; a novel universe swelling into existence, and then subsiding into nothingness, at every throb of the heart divine?

And now – this heart divine – what is it? It is our own.

Let not the merely seeming irreverence of this idea frighten our souls from that cool exercise of consciousness, from that deep tranquillity of self-inspection through which alone we can hope to attain the presence of this, the most sublime of truths, and look it leisurely in the face. The phenomena on which our conclusions must at this point depend are merely spiritual shadows, but nonetheless thoroughly substantial.

We walk about, amid the destinies of our world-existence, encompassed by dim but ever-present memories of a destiny more vast – very distant in the bygone time, and infinitely awful.

We live out a youth peculiarly haunted by such shadows, yet never mistaking them for dreams. As memories we know them. During our youth the distinction is too clear to deceive us even for a moment.

So long as this youth endures, the feeling that we exist is the most natural of all feelings. We understand it thoroughly. That there was a period at which we did not exist – or, that it might so have happened that we never had existed at all – are the considerations, indeed, which during this youth we find difficulty in understanding. Why we should not exist is, up to the epoch of manhood, of all queries the most unanswerable.

Existence – self-existence – existence from all time and to all eternity – seems, up to the epoch of manhood, a normal and unquestionable condition. *Seems*, because it is.

But now comes the period at which a conventional world-reason awakens us from the truth of our dream. Doubt, surprise, and incomprehensibility arrive at the same moment. They say: 'You live, and the time was when you lived not. You have been created. An intelligence exists greater than your own, and it is only through this intelligence that you live at all.' These things we struggle to comprehend and cannot – *cannot* because these things, being untrue, are thus of necessity incomprehensible.

No thinking being lives who, at some luminous point of his life of thought, has not felt himself lost amid the surges of futile efforts at understanding or believing that anything exists greater than his own soul. The utter impossibility of any one soul feeling itself inferior to another; the intense, overwhelming dissatisfaction and rebellion at the thought – these, with the omniprevalent aspirations at perfection, are but the spiritual, coincident with the material, struggles towards the original unity. They are, to my mind at least, a species of proof far surpassing what man terms demonstration, that no one soul is inferior to another, that nothing is, or can be, superior to any one soul, that each soul is, in part, its own God – its own creator. In a word, that God – the material and spiritual God – now exists solely in the diffused matter and spirit of the universe, and the regathering of this diffused matter and spirit will be but the reconstitution of the purely spiritual and individual God.

In this view, and in this view alone, we comprehend the riddles of divine injustice – of inexorable fate. In this view alone the existence of evil becomes intelligible; but in this view it becomes more – it becomes endurable. Our souls no longer rebel at a sorrow which we ourselves have imposed upon ourselves in furtherance of our own purposes, with a view – if even with a futile view – to the extension of our own joy.

I have spoken of memories that haunt us during our youth. They sometimes pursue us even into our manhood, assume gradually less and less indefinite shapes, now and then speak to us with low voices, saying:

'There was an epoch in the night of time, when a still-existent being existed – one of an absolutely infinite number of similar beings that people the absolutely infinite domains of the absolutely infinite space.[23] It was not and is not in the power of this being, any more than it is in your own, to extend by actual increase the joy of His existence. But just as it is in your power to expand or to concentrate your pleasures (the absolute amount of happiness remaining always the same), so did and does a similar capability appertain to this divine being, who thus passes his eternity in perpetual variation of concentrated self and almost infinite self-diffusion. What you call the universe of stars is but His present expansive existence. He now feels his life through an infinity of imperfect pleasures, the partial and pain-intertangled pleasures of those inconceivably numerous things which you designate as His creatures, but which are really but infinite individualisations of Himself. All these creatures – all – those which you term animate, as well as those to which you deny life for no better reason than that you do not behold it in operation – all these creatures have, in a greater or less degree, a capacity for pleasure and for pain, but the general sum of their sensations is precisely that amount of happiness which appertains by right to the divine being when concentrated within Himself. These creatures are all, too, more or less conscious intelligences – conscious, first, of a proper identity; conscious, secondly, and by faint indeterminate glimpses, of an identity with the divine being of whom we speak, of an identity with God. Of the two classes of consciousness, fancy that the former will grow weaker, the latter stronger, during the long succession of ages which must elapse before these myriads of individual intelligences become blended – when the bright stars become blended – into one. Think that the sense of individual identity will be gradually merged in the general consciousness; that man, for example, ceasing imperceptibly to feel himself man, will at length attain that awfully triumphant epoch when he shall recognise his existence as that of Jehovah. In the meantime bear in mind that all is life – life – life within life – the less within the greater, and all within the spirit divine."[24]

1. Show this in another edition. [Poe's manuscript note]

2. Schehallien in Wales. [Poe's manuscript note]

3. *The Murders in the Rue Morgue.* [Poe's manuscript note]

4. Here describe the process as one instantaneous flash. [Poe's manuscript note]

5. Succinctly, the surfaces of spheres are as the squares of their radii. [Poe's note]

6. See earlier paragraph, 'I reply that they do; as will be distinctly…' (p. 32) [Poe's note]

7. A sphere is necessarily limited. I prefer tautology to a chance of misconception. [Poe's note]

8. Caoutchouc is natural rubber that has not been vulcanised.

9. Laplace assumed his nebulosity heterogeneous, merely that he might be thus enabled to account for the breaking-up of the rings; for had the nebulosity been homogenous, they would not have broken. I reach the same result (heterogeneity of the secondary masses immediately resulting from the atoms) purely from a-priori consideration of their general design, relation. [Poe's note]

10. When this book went to press, the ring of Neptune had not been positively determined. [Poe's manuscript note]

11. Another asteroid (the text formerly read eight) discovered since the work went to press. [Poe's manuscript note]

12. I am prepared to show that the anomalous revolution of the satellites of Uranus is simply a perspective anomaly arising from the *bouleversement* of the axis of the planet. [Poe's note]

13. See earlier paragraph: 'With the understanding of a sphere of atoms…' (p. 50) [Poe's note]

14. See earlier paragraph: 'To electricity – so, for the present, continuing to call it…' (p. 27) [Poe's note]

15. *Views of the Architecture of the Heavens.* A letter, purporting to be from Dr Nichol to a friend in America, went the rounds of our newspapers, about two years ago [approx. 1846], I think, admitting 'the necessity' to which I refer. In a subsequent lecture, however, Dr Nichol appears in some manner to have gotten the better of the necessity, and does not quite *renounce* the theory, although he seems to wish that he could sneer at it as 'a purely hypothetical one'. What else was the law of gravity before the Maskelyne experiments? And who questioned the law of gravity, even then? The late experiments of Comte, however, are to the Laplacian theory what those of Maskelyne were to the Newtonian. [Poe's note]

16. It is not impossible that some unlooked-for optical improvement may disclose to us, among innumerable varieties of systems, a luminous sun, encircled by luminous and non-luminous rings, within and without and between which, revolve luminous and non-luminous planets, attended by moons having moons – and even these latter again having moons. [Poe's note]

17. *Mellonta tauta* (or 'These are the things the future may hold') is also the title of a short story by Poe, which was published in 1850.

18. See earlier paragraph: 'Now, to what does so partial a consideration tend...'
(p. 29) [Poe's note]

19. See Note 11.

20. I must be understood as denying, especially, only the revolutionary portion of Mädler's hypothesis. Of course, if no great central orb exists now in our cluster, such will exist hereafter. Whenever existing, it will be merely the nucleus of the consolidation. [Poe's note]

21. See p. 27 [Poe's note]

22. 'Gravity, then, must be the strongest of forces.' See p. 43 [Poe's note]

23. See pages 75, 76, paragraph commencing 'I reply that the "right" ', and ending 'proper and particular God.' [Poe's note]

24. The pain of the consideration that we shall lose our individual identity ceases at once when we further reflect that the process, as above described, is neither more or less than the absorption by each individual intelligence of all other intelligences (that is, of the universe) into its own. That God may be all in all, each must become God. [Poe's note]

Edgar Allan Poe was born in 1809 in Boston, Massachusetts, the son of itinerant actors. He was orphaned at the age of two and taken into the home of John Allan, a tobacco merchant. (It was from John Allan that Poe took his middle name.) They moved to England in 1815 where Poe attended school in Stoke Newington, an experience he later depicted in his imaginative story, 'William Wilson' (1839). He then returned to America to take up a place at the University of Virginia, but heavy debts forced him to leave after only a year. He entered the Military Academy at West Point in 1830 but this was again short lived and he was dishonourably discharged in 1831 following neglect of his duties.

Poe's early writings, including three volumes of verse, went largely unrecognised, and he was forced to earn his living working as a newspaper editor in Richmond, Philadelphia and New York. He took up lodgings with a relative, and in 1836 married her young daughter – his cousin, Virginia. However, like much of his life, this too was beset by tragedy when she died from tuberculosis eleven years later.

One of his most famous works, the Gothic romance 'The Fall of the House of Usher', appeared in 1840, but it was not until the publication of *The Raven and Other Poems* in 1845 that he gained renown as a writer. Despite the success of this and many other of his macabre and chilling tales, he continued to struggle with alcohol and depression until his death in Baltimore in 1849.

## HESPERUS PRESS – 100 PAGES

Hesperus Press, as suggested by the Latin motto, is committed to bringing near what is far – far both in space and time. Works written by the greatest authors, and unjustly neglected or simply little known in the English-speaking world, are made accessible through new translations and a completely fresh editorial approach. Through these short classic works, each little more than 100 pages in length, the reader will be introduced to the greatest writers from all times and all cultures.

For more information on Hesperus Press, please visit our website: **www.hesperuspress.com**

To place an order, please contact:
*Grantham Book Services*, Isaac Newton Way
Alma Park Industrial Estate
Grantham, Lincolnshire NG31 9SD
Tel: +44 (0) 1476 541080 Fax: +44 (0) 1476 541061
Email: orders@gbs.tbs-ltd.co.uk

## SELECTED TITLES FROM HESPERUS PRESS

Gustave Flaubert *Memoirs of a Madman*
Alexander Pope *Scriblerus*
Ugo Foscolo *Last Letters of Jacopo Ortis*
Anton Chekhov *The Story of a Nobody*
Joseph von Eichendorff *Life of a Good-for-nothing*
Mark Twain *The Diary of Adam and Eve*
Giovanni Boccaccio *Life of Dante*
Victor Hugo *The Last Day of a Condemned Man*
Joseph Conrad *Heart of Darkness*
Emile Zola *For a Night of Love*
Daniel Defoe *The King of Pirates*
Giacomo Leopardi *Thoughts*
Nikolai Gogol *The Squabble*

Franz Kafka *Metamorphosis*
Herman Melville *The Enchanted Isles*
Leonardo da Vinci *Prophecies*
Charles Baudelaire *On Wine and Hashish*
William Makepeace Thackeray *Rebecca and Rowena*
Wilkie Collins *Who Killed Zebedee?*
Théophile Gautier *The Jinx*
Charles Dickens *The Haunted House*
Luigi Pirandello *Loveless Love*
Fyodor Dostoevsky *Poor People*
E.T.A. Hoffmann *Mademoiselle de Scudéri*
Henry James *In the Cage*
Francesco Petrarch *My Secret Book*
D.H. Lawrence *The Fox*
Percy Bysshe Shelley *Zastrozzi*